The Love You Crave

A Course in Ascension, Alchemy, and Connection to the Divine

WAXÉLA SANANDA

Copyright

For Josiah; you have been inspiring me since the day I learned you were coming into this world. You make the world a better place.

And for Gabriel; you keep me grounded and bring me so much laughter. I am so proud of you both!

Table of Contents

Affirmation of Receiving the Activation Codes

I receive the divine codes
I activate the divine codes within and through me
I am the light, I am the frequency, I am the Source of divinity, I am the Christ Consciousness
Christis
I activate Ascension through my heart
Through the diamond light portal of the ascended heart
We will all ascend to a higher platform through this frequency
I bring the frequency to this reality, construct platform through my being here now
This is my mission, the activation of this dimension, the Ascension of this dimension
It is why I came here now
I choose to activate fully now
I am the light
I am the way
I am the Christ Codes
I am the Oneness
Ascension is *now*
In 5D and higher
I Am

CHAPTER 1:

Why Do I Feel so Lonely?

There is an inner loneliness that lies just below the surface of your personality. You can go about your day at work, to and from your children's school, even while at home with your family, and you ignore it. You act as if it isn't there. You pretend it isn't eating away at you because you are ok, you have a good (enough) life. You have enough food enough money to pay your bills. You have a car or a way to get around and a place to live. You have a family, people love you. "I shouldn't feel lonely or disconnected," you tell yourself. "I should be happy. I have everything I need. People would beg to have my life."

But something is missing. It is something deep but hidden, veiled so you can't put your finger on it.

You want love. You crave love. You are starving for it. Even if you are in a relationship, and even if it's a good relationship, you want more love. Maybe you've found yourself thinking, "If I had a spiritual partner or if my partner was more into practicing spirituality, maybe then we could connect and I wouldn't feel so lonely."

The reality is that you can't change your partner, and if you are single and wishing for a partner to fill that loneliness gap you feel, there are a few things that need to happen before that will work.

There is never a convenient time to work on yourself. I realize you may have responsibilities like kids, families, clients, work, physical issues, money concerns, or some combination of all of these and more. There are so many reasons not to do it. But what about that feeling of emptiness? The feeling like something or someone is missing. What about that nagging angst in the depth of your gut that keeps telling you there is more?

Are you trying to tune it out with work, food, wine, sex, social media, video games, or possibly with healthy things like exercise, an extreme diet, or hours upon hours of meditation? If you are doing any of these things and still feeling that undercurrent of melancholy, that drive is telling you something is missing, this book can help you.

I've been there; I know that feeling well. I've tried to drown it with alcohol, drugs, relationships, meditation, spirituality, art, reading, food, and I even played Candy Crush addictively for four years trying to numb that feeling. Even though it seemed to be just a dull ache, it was, at times, unbearable. I didn't know how to get away from it. It was *in* me, consuming me, and I was *stuck* with it.

I could have stayed where I was and kept numbing myself. I was "okay" (at least, I appeared to be from the outside looking in). I could have stayed small, invisible, pretending that everything was fine. But while I was spending years checking out, life was passing. My kids were growing up, the life I was born to live was missing me, and I was missing it!

So, let me ask you this... are you happy? Are you deeply happy, fulfilled to the depth of your soul happy? Are you living your purpose in a grand way, driven by your inner mission, not from the void within, but fulfilled from your deepest truth?

If you are, that is great! I am celebrating with you! Use this book to amplify that feeling and become more activated, aligned, and successful. But if you aren't, isn't it time to find out why?

I finally got courageous enough to get real with myself and break through. I broke through the pain and the melancholy and the anger and the self-loathing, and I changed. I did it, and I know that you can too.

I *honor* all of your pain, all that has happened and that is currently happening. I realize your life is probably busy. Maybe you are thinking you don't have the time, the money, the will-power, etcetera… but what is it costing you to stay where you are? What is it costing you *not* to address that feeling of loneliness deep within your soul? Whether you realize it or not, it is damaging your relationships with family and friends. If you have children, they can feel it in you and they are being influenced by it. It is causing you to feel anxious and uncentered, it is keeping you from fulfilling your purpose, from trusting yourself, and from feeling contentment and peace. The void within you is sucking up your most valuable asset: your time here in this body, in this life. It is inevitably taking a toll on your health and wellbeing, and it's keeping you from feeling whole.

Take this journey with me and I will guide you through a process of addressing the shadow within you that is stealing your light. You will arrive at the end feeling whole and complete as a sovereign being. You will no longer feel the yearning desire for someone to complete you. You will understand and embody your purpose, and you can and will have the empowering, fulfilling relationship(s) you desire.

Your life will finally make sense, your purpose will become clear, your spiritual gifts will come online, and you will no longer feel alone.

Isn't it time to live your *best* life *now? The only time to say *yes* to yourself and your growth is *now* because now is the only time you have.

I know that stepping up can be painful and even scary. Releasing habits, people, and comfortable things can be difficult, releasing old ideas and replacing them with new ones requires courage in the face of fear. I understand, and I believe in you. I know you can do it, because I did it, and I'm continuing to do it. We can do it together.

"If it doesn't scare you, you're not dreaming big enough!"

Let's dream *BIG!*

CHAPTER 2:

ET's, a Shaman, and Collecting Soul Codes

Indigenous cultures use verbal storytelling as a way to share information, inspiration and wisdom. Stories also hold encoded information that can trigger awakenings and openings in the reader or listener. It is my intention that sharing some of my awakening stories with you will open a door in your awareness and receptivity and that you will gain an understanding of how even the play we engage in as children is grooming us for the life and mission we are here to live.

First Encounter

I was three years old, lying in my bed. I could hear my mother in the bathroom down the hall getting ready for bed, and that was comforting, just knowing that she was nearby. I was beginning to drift off into that sweet space between awake and asleep when there was a light at my window. That was odd because I had a second-story bedroom and the car lights didn't show through. I also lived in a rural neighborhood in Iowa, the last house at the top of a small hill, so there was no traffic, especially at night.

But a light was at my window after bedtime. The next thing I saw was beyond my understanding. Even at that young age, when I hadn't fully developed my rational mind, I knew something out of the ordinary was going on.

There was a very strange looking man at my window. He looked more like an insect than a man, but he was wearing a uniform and he was busy doing something. I felt an unusual pressure around my body which made me yell, but I had no voice, and I couldn't move! I fought against the "pressure" I was feeling and my whole body was prickly, you know the feeling of pins and needles you get when your foot goes to sleep? That feeling encompassed my whole body, and I fought against it until I rolled over the side of my bed. Something even stranger happened then. I stuck to the side of my bed feeling suction and that prickly energy when I should have fallen to the floor! That was so unexpected that I stopped fighting and observed the experience. At some point, the energy abruptly stopped and I dropped to the floor. I was bewildered and confused, having no idea what had happened, and I crawled back in bed with the idea in my mind "Don't tell the adults, they won't understand."

I slept peacefully and deeply after that, and I didn't remember much about it the next day. But the idea not to tell the adults stuck with me for many years, into my own adult life. I had many more experiences like this one, that I vaguely remembered, and consequently, I was terrified to sleep alone at night.

About twenty-five years later, I met Joren, a hypnosis practitioner who did hypnotic regression using QHHT (Quantum Healing Hypnosis Technique). He helped me revisit the entire scene that I could only remember bits of consciously.

Under hypnosis, I was able to go right back into the experience and relive it as if I was observing it in real-time. I met the "Insectoid" who I recalled seeing at my window. He was a biped cricket being (which explains my uncanny fear of crickets) and I interviewed him about the happenings of this event.

From this perspective, I was able to see that there was some sort of power cord coming through the window. It looked like an etheric shimmering tube that connected to something unseen outside the window, and to a large cocoon-like capsule that the young me was inside of. The cricket man told me that this was a pre-incarnational agreement, that the power cord was connecting me to the "council of light," and that on this cord, I was able to send and receive information. "This was all agreed upon before you came here," he assured me.

The cocoon was like a charging station. That prickly energy that I was feeling was an infusion of light, energy, and information that I was going to need for my mission. I would be tapped into this energy for the duration of my time on the planet.

I asked him how the cord was used and he showed me that it is like a USB plug into an energy source, as if my council was a computer and I was a flash drive. I could download as needed from Source, and the Council could upload my experiences. That explained a lot for me since I continue to get downloads of energy and information on a regular basis.

I know now that it all comes from within me, but the perception is that it comes from somewhere "higher." Higher may mean an ascended dimension, a higher frequency, or a higher vibration. Whatever it means, I can tap in, turn on, and feel and receive from it on demand.

I am now practicing embodying higher frequencies, the Christ Consciousness frequencies, moving ever closer to the *Oneness*, and I feel the frequencies working with me. I activate others into the codes, the frequencies, and help them run energy through their bodies, their nervous systems, and their energy fields.

These are frequencies that people can be attuned to. I received them by attuning to my higher consciousness, from working with and channeling Isis, from Christis, who I know as the feminine voice of Christ Consciousness, from meditation and breathwork, and the power cord attached to my council of light. Ultimately all of these frequencies come from and lead to Source, Oneness, the collective WHOLE.

If you are open to receiving the Activation codes and aligning with the ascension frequencies that are here, ready and available to all who desire to receive them, go to the beginning of the book, just after the table of contents, and read the **Affirmation of Receiving the Activation Codes.** Read the affirmation, contemplate the meaning, and if it feels right in your heart, consciously open your heart to receive. This is a personal process. I have made you aware of the codes and the opportunity you have to receive them, but it must be your personal choice to open to receive them. Sit with them, feel them, experience them on your own terms. And when you are ready, let them in. This is not a one time experience, but rather an ongoing opening with layers of possibility. You will receive what you are open to and ready for. Tomorrow or next week you may open to new codes. It is an unfolding that continues, and as you expand and grow, so does your ability to receive. As you receive more, you naturally have more to give. You begin to overflow with the essence of life, and you will want to share it. Then others will receive the codes from you, and they will expand and overflow and share, and this is how we raise the frequency of this entire reality. It begins with you. You are the light and Ascension is *now*.

The Swamp

I was seven years old riding my red, white, and blue bicycle. I had an empty, plastic, one-gallon ice cream tub, complete with lid and red handle in the basket in front of my glittery, tassel adorned handlebars. I was on my way to "the swamp" as I affectionately called my marshy childhood playground. I loved the swamp. The gatekeepers of the entrance were seven giant weeping willow trees with branches so long that they brushed the ground, creating a fort-like fortress where I could park my bike and enter unseen into the wetland. Next, I would tunnel through the tall grass. In the summer months, it would grow taller than me, swallowing me up with its bushy green splendor as I trekked my way toward the murky water's edge. The towering cattails gave way to the clearing that harbored what was no more than a large pond but felt to me like an endless sea. I would emerge, ice cream bucket in hand with pre-cut holes in the lid, and I was home. This is where I felt at one with everything around me. All of nature spoke to me here and I would lose myself in the joy of being.

This is where I became still. Completely motionless. I would quiet and slow my breath for intervals while I "tuned in" to the miniature world at my ankles. I would stand there in the beginning, unable to see the fairyland at my feet. But soon, the landscape would transform, my vision would shift, and an entire world would open up below me that I was now a giant observer of, and I was able to stand there, undetected, watching in fascination, the busy buzzing supercity of insects and amphibious creatures.

I was on a mission to catch frogs. I had no real reason for wanting frogs aside from the challenge of catching them, filling my bucket, returning home with them, and later letting them go. I would stand motionless at the edge of the water watching, and when my vision had fully shifted, I could see them... before they saw me. Before my vision shifted, they would see me and jump in the water before I could get close, before I was even aware of their presence. But after I tuned in, they became shiny beacons shimmering in gold and green iridescence. Even when a frog was sitting completely still, I could see its heart beating, and occasionally a tongue would shoot out so fast to surprise and consume a passing insect. Then they were easy for me to catch. I pounced quickly, like a young cat, and in the bucket they went. When I had four or five frogs and a couple of salamanders I would hike back out to my bike in the willows, gently place my bucket of treasures in my basket, and be on my way.

I didn't realize it then, but I learned (or perhaps remembered) how to meditate and control my breathing in my quest for frogs. I learned how to *tune out of one reality and tune in to another*. I learned that I could become invisible to the tiny world and move about unseen. It was so curious to me that the tiny world at the edge of the water was so alive and vital and fast compared to the large, metallic, heavy world that humans created. The vitality, energy, balance, and harmony just felt better. If I was ever having a down day, or just needed support, I would go sit with my back against one of the massive willow trees and let it drain away my frustration and restore my sense of belonging, of purpose. When I joined forces with the trees I was refreshed. They were my friends and nurturers. I always knew the willows were watching out for me when I was at the swamp. I could feel their spirits and their wisdom. I never felt alone or afraid, I knew I was connected and protected.

I'm not sure when it happened, but somewhere along my journey from childhood to teenager, I closed off my extrasensory intuition, my empathic ability to feel everything, the trees, the environment, and other people's emotions. I was an empath, but life can be rough and overwhelming and I put up walls. The boundaries kept me from feeling too much. They also kept me from noticing too much of the pain in the world, and helped me live in my little bubble, safe and protected yet not nearly as connected. I was comfortable in my little bubble world, and I wasn't even aware that I was in a bubble... until it popped.

The Mayan

I applied and was chosen to be a foreign exchange student after I graduated from high school. I was only seventeen, and it seemed like a great way to learn about the world. I was chosen to go to Merida, Mexico for Prepatoria, their thirteenth year of school between high school and college.

Aside from family vacations, I hadn't spent any time outside of Iowa, so this was a big expansion opportunity for me. My year in the Yucatan was full of challenges, trials, and tribulations, but the real expansion happened when I visited the Mayan ruins. I was invited to Chichen Itza first. I loved everything about it. The pyramids, the sculptures, the art, the tiny stairs. I felt comfortable there, even though I knew little to nothing about the Mayan culture before that. I became obsessed with the Mayan ruins and I went to as many as possible, every chance I got. Uxmal, Tulum, The Lol-Tun Caves... I soaked them in. There was an energy in the Mayan ruins that I didn't understand at the time, but I felt it. I felt connected there, the way I did back at home in the swamp.

That year turned out to be the year of my spiritual awakening. It was the year I realized there was something beyond myself directing my life. I felt things, knew things, perceived things that were beyond my usual, 3D awareness. I know now that I was picking up "soul codes" in the Mayan ruins. The ruins held encoded information that I had stored there for myself, and these codes activated me in to an experience of life beyond the third dimension and reactivated my spiritual gifts. My life would have a very different drive and focus after that. I began to understand the world of energy and frequency as I was downloading information from other aspects of myself beyond the known. I began to see clairvoyantly again and to empathically feel other people, places, and energies.

Many years after my Mayan experiences in the Yucatan, I was guided to visit Tikal, the Mayan ruins in Guatemala, where I hiked up to the top of the north pyramid. There I was greeted by a Mayan princess named Ke-Bah who told me she was expecting me and that the council was waiting for me. She told me she was the inner earth Mayan expression of myself and she took me to a council of elders where I was able to ask any questions I desired. I was unaware of how long I spent in this timeless dimension with Ke-Bah and the council. When I returned to the top of the pyramid, it was nearing dusk, and I hiked out before sunset, grateful that I had received everything I had come for and more.

The Shaman

In my early twenties, I was living with my boyfriend in an artist's community called Moon Mansion in Dallas, Texas. I was the owner of a unique little gift shop called "Psychedelic Situation" on lower Greenville Avenue. I encountered many interesting people and I continued to deepen and expand in my spiritual awakening during that time.

That was the year that my guidance began inserting Kauai, Hawaii into my daily life. I would hear about it from a friend, from a random shopper in my store that would start telling me about an experience they had in Kauai, and even though I rarely watched TV, I would hear news from Kauai when I turned one on. One day, a magazine mysteriously appeared on my desk with an article about the Napali coast trail in Kauai... the synchronicities were undeniable. I knew I had to go to Kauai.

I was in the process of arranging a trip to Kauai when I started hearing about a shaman that was visiting the area. Several different sources told me I needed to meet him, and that he somehow made them think

THE LOVE YOU CRAVE

of me when they heard him speak, although no one could say why.

I arrived at Moon Mansion one evening after leaving my shop and my boyfriend told me that a shaman was at the next-door neighbor's apartment and that I should go meet him. It was the shaman I had been hearing about. I spent the evening in conversation with him. At the end of the evening, the shaman told me he was planning to go to Kauai and he asked me to travel there with him. I arranged my life to be in Kauai for three months, and I ended up staying for three years. During that time with the shaman, I learned to deepen and expand my spiritual abilities. He had complete and open access to the multidimensional Akashic records at all times, and traveling with him was a dream come true for me with my endless questions about life beyond 3D reality. I was deep in training for the time I was with him.

And then he was gone. The body he had inhabited was still present, but it wasn't him. He was no longer present in that body. I was confused at that time, but years later, my guidance showed me what had happened. The shaman was a *walk-in* spirit. He was my twin flame from a higher dimension and he appeared in my life to train me in my spiritual gifts, to assist me in my awakening, and to prepare me for my service and mission going forward. The body he was in had a near-death experience in a drug overdose. The man in that body took time out of the body in the spirit realm to recover. The shaman repaired and recovered the health of his host body while teaching me and others, and when the body had regained its wellness and the original owner of the body had regained his emotional stability the exchange was made. It was all arranged before we came into this incarnation. When I had completed my training and his body was recovered enough for the original personality to come back in, my twin flame shaman retreated, and I was left with a companion that I didn't relate to. The lessons I learned changed my life and opened my mind to the multidimensionality that we are an expression of here on this planet, in these bodies.

My life has been full of mystical experiences. I like to move at a fast pace, I'm great at starting things, and when I get bored, I jump ship. That has been both my strong suit and my downfall. If I'm not expanding, I'm contracting. I have a voracious appetite for personal growth and transformation. I used to expect the people around me to have the same insatiable desire to explore themselves and the multidimensionality of reality, and when they didn't, the relationship would suffer. I know now that my journey is not validated or invalidated by anyone else's. I am much more forgiving and generous now in my relationships than I was then. I have learned not to expect so much, as well as not to take anything personally. I have become the source of my validation and sovereignty. I no longer need the world to feed me the answers because I know how to access them from within. I have gained access to my wholeness and completeness. I have found the joy of *being*. And from there my relationships have become a source of joy, fun, exploration, curiosity, and communion.

I no longer feel the need to stay quiet because the "adults won't understand." I know that this is my time for visibility and speaking the wholeness of my truth.

I have been given the gift of carrying the *Ascension Codes*, awakening frequencies that assist others in remembering who they are, to inspire others to wake up to a greater knowing of themselves as divine beings embodied in human technology. My journey has been one of incessant expansion. It hasn't always been easy or convenient, but it has been worth the effort. I now get to share all that I have learned and remembered in my Ascension Training, guiding clients into their truth, their purpose, and the embodiment of their Divinity. It is my greatest joy to see the success of my clients as they unfold into their expansion.

I have a lifetime of experiences that have molded me into a channel of light. My purpose and my service now are to share that light with those who choose to receive it, and together as a community of lightworkers we will enlighten this world.

CHAPTER 3:

———————

The Journey to Wholeness

T his book is going to take you on a journey that will start with your mind and end with your body.

You will become aware of the programs you have been running that have kept you feeling alone and in the shadows rather than playing big and shining bright like the sun.

It is good to follow the steps laid out in each chapter sequentially first, and once you understand how each step works, you can practice the tools you have learned as needed in your daily life. This book is full of tools and technologies that, once you become familiar with them and you learn to use them with some confidence, you will have them forever. The best way to get the most out of what you learn here is to create a practice, a daily regimen of implementing what you learned every day and using it in your day to day life. The only way you won't get results is if you read the book and don't utilize the tools in it. I can give you all of the information you need, but it is up to you to use it. You must take responsibility for your success, in these chapters and in your life. Tenacity, consistency, curiosity, and baby steps each day will lead you to massive breakthroughs in due time.

We begin by working with your mindset and the mental programming you need to upgrade in order to attract what you desire. When you have upgraded your mindset and recognized where many of your limiting beliefs began, you will have a new outlook on the world and how you can change your perception by changing your thinking.

As we move into working with your shadow programming, recognizing what your triggers are, and releasing their hold on you, you will begin to feel lighter, happier, and more connected.

From there, I will teach you a very specific way to recode your shadow programs, and upgrade your mind, body, and spirit. I call it RHOS (recoding the human operating system), and you will learn to use it to upgrade your frequency, your thoughts, feelings, behavior, and your life.

Resistance is a universal program that keeps us from realizing our potential. Working through resistance and surrendering control is a crucial step on your path to wholeness. You will learn that releasing the resistance that has kept you in anxiety and fear will bring you a level of freedom that you didn't know you could access. Through surrendering and opening to the world of higher consciousness, you will expand.

Feeling what you feel rather than avoiding, hiding, diverting, or resisting is a big step toward embodying higher frequencies. You will learn to embody what you are feeling, and this experience will allow you to upgrade your nervous system, repair your DNA, and receive the Ascension frequencies in your daily meditations.

We live in a society that values knowledge above feeling: the mind over the heart. Wisdom is precious, but one can only become truly wise when knowledge is more than mental. It must also be felt and assimilated in the heart. The heart is an infinite portal that you will learn to open to a greater extent. You will have access to attune to the frequency of the heart and learn to journey within. There are no limits to where you can travel and what you can learn through the infinite portal of the heart.

Whether you are in a relationship or not, I know you are looking for deep, soul-fulfilling love. You will learn how to shift your energy to become a "match" to your soul mate or twin flame.

Finally, you will become spiritually activated and experience deeply fulfilling wholeness and love.

You will tap into the realm of divine bliss, embodying very high-frequency states, and this embodiment makes you irresistible to all that you desire.

If you are ready to experience the love that you have been craving while becoming more mystical, more heart-centered, and reaching new levels of freedom and connection to the Divine, buckle your seatbelt! The journey begins now.

CHAPTER 4:

Managing Your Mindset

Who thought that? You know that thought. The one behind the one you are conscious of thinking? What about the thought behind that? If you sit quietly with your mind for a moment, can you get a sense of the layers of thought that are swirling around in your mind?

Try it. Try sitting quietly for one minute and think of nothing. Just sit and notice what is happening in your mind.

What happened?

My bet is that you found thoughts that you didn't realize were there. There were thoughts that you were consciously thinking, like "this is silly," and "I need to move the clothes from the washing machine to the dryer."

Did you also find thoughts that came from somewhere else? If not, try it again for longer this time and just notice. There are layers of thoughts in your mind. Some of them are yours; these are often helpful thoughts like your to-do list. You can use this part of your mind to consciously think positive thoughts. For instance, you may be familiar with reciting affirmations. Maybe you do daily affirmations where you consciously tell yourself that you are great, smart, beautiful, thin, perfect, etcetera. Affirmations are great, but they don't work if you are running counter thoughts at a deeper level of your subconscious. These are the layers of thought I am asking you to notice. You have many layers of thinking, which I also refer to as programming, and your reality is being run mostly by the inner programming, the subconscious thoughts that you aren't aware of.

It is the subconscious thinking that can sabotage your life and your efforts to succeed. If you have tried and failed a number of times at something you desire to achieve, you are most likely running a destructive program in that area.

Where did these thoughts come from and what can I do about it?

We will be diving deeply into what you can do about those subconscious thoughts once you learn to recognize the programming that put them there. Some of your programming is inherited from your parents or the people who raised you. As children, we are like sponges. We download programs from the people around us. This is how we survived as a species, and it is still very useful when we are surrounded by positive messages, such as how smart, ambitious, and creative we are. Unfortunately, no matter what kind of messages you were surrounded by as a child, you inevitably picked up some negative programming that is sabotaging your ultimate success in life. The reason that all of those affirmations you've been rehearsing haven't become the truth of your reality is because of these underlying programs that you are unaware of.

There are programs that come with our genetic lineage, society, our past lives, our starseed lineage, as well as programs we pick up like viruses from watching the news or TV *programs* (that word is not an accident; you are being programmed every time you watch TV).

There are programs that you downloaded from the kids you went to daycare, elementary school, middle school, high school, and college with. Your teachers programmed you. You are running programs upon programs upon programs. These are the layers. Some are helping you succeed and others are blocking your success.

Wouldn't it be nice if you could laser-focus on the programs that are sabotaging you and reprogram them to be supportive? That is the alchemy of reprogramming the human operating system. The body you own is a magnificent technology that didn't come with an operator's manual. This book is the guide, the reprogramming manual that can take you from self-sabotage to Ascension if you follow the process.

I believe in you. I know you can do this, and that you are ready for it because you found this book. Something about this work called to you and here you are, downloading the new programming that you need to succeed in life. Congratulations on embarking on this inward journey of transformation!

So, what about diseases? What if you have a parent or family "gene" for cancer? If you are subconsciously running the cancer program, you are going to get cancer too. Not because of your genes; you have *all* of the genes inside your human tech, including those that have cancer tendencies and those that do not. It's the programs that you are running that signal the cancer program to turn on or off.

This is a very good reason to take note of your subconscious programming and start to recode your mind, isn't it? You have the control to run the program or not or to stop the program even if it has already begun. You have to take on your mind, your thoughts, and your programming and diligently work with it, and you can recreate your body and your mind, you can free yourself from anxiety, you can release yourself from the programs that cause you to be ill. You can also turn on the programs that cause you to attract what you want. You can become so magnetically attractive to your desires that they can't help but manifest in your life. You can even do this for love and your soulmate or twin flame relationship. But you have some work to do first, so let's get to it!

Upgrading Your Mindset

Now that you are aware that there are programs running your reality, you are ready for some tools to begin to find and become aware of the programming you want to upgrade. You can't work with a belief, shadow program, or sabotaging thought if you don't know it exists. This is why so many people fail to manifest their dreams and also why they fail after creating a big success in life. If you have shadow programs that you aren't aware of and you don't work with them and you have a big success, those programs will find a way to take you down unless you work with them and release them. Once you have found your shadow programs and done the work to identify, feel, and release them, I will show you how you can take it to the next level to recode them in order to have an upgraded program running *in favor of* your success.

I will get into the step-by-step process of this in the next chapter. That is where we will deep dive into finding your dark programs. But there are many ways to begin this work right now. Neville Goddard is an author who I admire deeply. He teaches how to use visualization and the feeling experience to manifest your reality.

> "Change your conception of yourself and you will automatically change the world in which you live. Do not try to change people; they are only messengers telling you who you are. Revalue yourself and they will confirm theW change."
> — Neville Goddard

Perception-Based Reality

Your thoughts create your reality. This world is a matrix that we perceive through the lens of our own mind, our beliefs, our energetic frequency, and yes, our shadow programs all combine to give us the experience of life that we are generating internally. It truly is all within you! You have the power to create and destroy. You are the one responsible for everything you are experiencing. The human experience is truly the most incredible and sacred gift. It is a school, a university for learning that what we think, feel, and how we behave impacts all of life, particularly our own. This life is your opportunity to experience anything and everything you desire to experience. You get to choose. If you want to experience abundance but you keep experiencing lack, congratulations! You have been running subconscious programming that has kept you in lack, and now that you are aware of it you can change it. There is so much power in that. It takes courage to change old programs. You have to be willing to look at the origin of where that lack program began and feel it, and release it. If you aren't courageous enough to look under that rug, where you buried those old thoughts and stuffed away those old programs, this won't work for you. You have to be willing to hunt for it, find it, feel it in the body, and release it for good. Then you get to upgrade it to a new code, recoding and alchemizing that program and turning it into the gold that you will build your future with.

Thoughts Getting Lodged in the Body

Did you know that your body holds thoughts and experiences in your cells, your bloodstream, your organs, your muscle tissues? Anywhere in the body can be a potential place for a program to get stuck.

A father and his son had the exact same scar on their right knee, which they each got at the same age. The son's scar appeared twenty-two years after the father's did. This is an example of a direct genetic lineage program manifesting as a physical characteristic of the body. The son inherited the program that would manifest as a scar on his knee and he played out a scenario to make it manifest, all subconsciously and as a result of an inherited genetic pattern (program) from his father and his father's lineage. Our thoughts get lodged in the body, and we can inherit the thought pattern, we can pick it up from living life, we can even bring it in from the womb or a past life. Regardless of where they originated, the good news is that there is a way to release these thoughts from the body.

Releasing Thoughts from the Body

Allow yourself at least twenty minutes of quiet, undisturbed time for this process. Turn off your phone and place it out of reach (make sure it is off so that it won't buzz and take you out of your process). If you live with children, your family, or anyone who might want your attention, let them know that you are taking the next twenty minutes to work on yourself and that you are not to be disturbed for any reason short of a major emergency. Put a "do not disturb" sign on your door to remind everyone.

Sit or lie down in a comfortable, quiet place.

Breathe deeply for several breaths to get present, centered, and calibrated to this present moment, here and now, in your body.

Breathe into your heart center and feel the energy of your heart.

Ask your body if it will cooperate with you. Ask it to speak to you and tell it you are ready to listen. This is a time of sacred communion with the body.

How often do you speak to your body and really listen to what it has to share with you? The body is a multidimensional warehouse of information. If you want to understand its secrets, you must tune into it and give it your full attention. When you do this, it will open and begin the process of revealing to you the great mysteries and the infinite wisdom it holds.

It is time now to scan your body. Begin with your heart and the area around your chest.

How does your heart feel? What sensations do you notice in your chest?

Listen to the rhythm of your heart beating. Breathe into this center and listen.

Ask your heart to guide you in scanning your body. The heart is a portal, and it knows exactly where you need to travel in your body and what you need to release.

Let your awareness be guided as you scan your body. You can do this from head to toe, from feet to the top of your head, or you can let your attention be drawn naturally to any area that is commanding your attention. If you feel pain, pulsing, tingling, heat, coolness, or any other type of sensation, energetic or physical, let your awareness go to that place and tune in. Ask your body to tell you what it needs and what it is holding in any area that your attention is drawn to.

Then listen. Listen with your multisensory being. This means you may or may not "hear" the body speaking; there any many ways the body can communicate with you. Pain is the most dramatic way; pain is the body's way of screaming for your attention. But if you can learn to hear your body's whispers, you will not need to feel pain because you will be able to give the body what it needs before pain is necessary.

Listen to the whispers. Feel what there is to feel. Don't try too hard to understand; let the body lead you. Ask and allow. Surrender to the rhythm and the messages your body has to share with you. You may begin to see images in your mind. You may be transported into a memory. Let these images and memories play out. They hold valuable information for you about what you have stored in your body. You may have a sudden or gradual knowingness. You may hear words or phrases. You may see symbols or fractals in your mind's eye. You may feel unusual sensations. Just allow whatever you experience to be exactly as it is. Go with it and persuade your body to continue. Any experience is valuable. If you have a history of ignoring your body, this may take several attempts. Think of it as establishing a new form of communication. You don't learn a new language in one session but you can learn a few new words. Be encouraged by whatever you discover. Thank your body for the feedback you received. Write down what you have learned, received, and discovered in your journal and ask to be shown the deeper meaning in your meditation or dreamtime.

Congratulate yourself! What you are doing can and will become the foundation of conscious communication with the deeper truth of who you are through your body. This is a powerful practice and I encourage you to do it daily.

I have recorded a guided meditation to assist you in this process which you can access through the website. https://waxelasananda.com/TLYC

When I began doing this work, I didn't realize how transformational it would be for me. This process saved me from what I am convinced would have become ovarian cancer if I had not found it and transformed it through this technique.

I woke up feeling an energy in my lower left abdominal area. As I tuned in, the sensation felt blocked and also a little crampy or achy. I asked my body where this was coming from and what I needed to know. I was guided to a memory of when I was sixteen years old. I went to a party on a double date with a girlfriend and two boys from another town. Neither of us had been out with those boys before. I ended up being date raped at that party. This was before anyone talked about date rape, and I had no idea how to deal with it so I didn't tell anyone. I internalized the experience and tried to pretend it didn't happen. I never saw that boy again. I've done the personal work of forgiving the boy and forgiving myself for getting into that situation. I had not thought of that event in many years. But while my mind had released that trauma, my body had held on to a piece of it and I could now feel a mass of energy in my left ovary. I could see the mass in my mind's eye, and now that I knew where it came from, I saw that I needed to continue to work with it and clear the energy there. I worked with that energy in my left ovary daily for two weeks. It started out (as I could see it in my mind's eye) as a yellow mass with the consistency of a gummy bear, soft but congealed. I could see that if left alone, it would have continued to harden and eventually it would have become a tumor, possibly even cancerous. Fortunately, I caught it before that happened. As I worked with it, I felt it losing density, day by day. It continued to lessen in density until it became a barely formed light ball of energy, and finally, after working with it for about two weeks, I felt it "pop" and it was gone. Now when I scan that area of my body, there is nothing left there that isn't positive energy.

I share this story because I know that many people have sexual traumas from their childhood and young adult life that need to be cleared from the physical body. The discomfort of remembering the origin of the trauma is much better than the discomfort of acquiring a disease or needing to have a mass surgically removed. It is also important to note that even if a cancerous tumor or a mass is removed if the energetic pattern of disharmony is not dealt with, it is very likely that the cancer will return either in the same place or in another area of the body. Even if you are a cancer survivor, I highly recommend doing this work to release the disharmonious energy that caused it. You can save yourself a relapse and your body will be much healthier for it.

It is important to note that trauma can also be inherited through genetic lineage. Even if you did not experience the trauma, in some cases you could still inherit a program from a trauma that occurred in your lineage, and for this reason it is beneficial to clear your body of all trauma across all time and space, and including all of your genetic and ancestral lineage.

Holding weight in the body is also often attached to embodied trauma. I found that after clearing my ovarian mass, it was easier for me to keep weight off my belly. If you are holding excess weight on your body, you can use this process to work through the embodied energies that are keeping the pounds on you. You can use the body scan and releasing technique described in this chapter in addition to the RHOS recoding technique in chapter 6 to release the weight and keep it off.

What about attracting love? How does mindset apply to finding the love, the soul mate, twin flame, or the deep connection in partnership you desire?

You will attract people and situations that are at the same frequency you are vibrating at. If you are looking for a love relationship and you have the feeling of "I can't find love," "I long for love," or if you are yearning for love, the energy you are putting out is one of longing, yearning, needing, and wanting. Therefore, what you will experience back is longing, yearning, needing, and wanting. This usually doesn't manifest a partner, but if it does, the partner you attract will reflect the attributes of longing and neediness, which may show up as a codependent relationship or a relationship void of trust because it was attracted from wanting something that you don't perceive you have.

The first step in mindset for attracting a healthy relationship is to focus on what you are satisfied with within yourself, just as you are, single and all. Even if you want a relationship more than anything in the world, there are things you can find about yourself that make you happy.

Start here. Focus on what you love about you. Write it down in your journal. Celebrate yourself. Just by honoring yourself, you will be raising your vibration and becoming more compatible with a great partner who also honors him/herself! Someone who has honed self-respect and love will have healthy boundaries and is much less likely to be jealous. The more you nurture your relationship with yourself, the more you become attractive to a mate, and ironically, you also become less consumed with needing one.

If you are so absorbed with wanting a partner that you get upset when you see happy couples together in public, this is an area you can go to work on immediately. You have to shift your thinking from envy to one of feeling happy for the joyful couples you encounter. When you can see a couple together, enjoying each other's company, imagine how that feels and how enjoyable it is to share your life with someone. Feel the positive feelings that you believe having a partner will bring you and generate a feeling of gratitude and celebration for the love you see in the world. This mental shift and physical experience of the feeling of satisfaction in a relationship will instantly begin to shift your frequency to one of compatibility with a partner who also celebrates love and life.

You can use this "Celebration Technique" for any trait you feel envious of in another person. If you feel resentful when you see a wealthy person driving your dream car, shift to celebrating for him or her, thoughts like, "He did it!", "That must be so awesome for her!", and "I bet it feels incredible!" are going to shift your frequency *up*, which is exactly what you want, while envious, resentful, or hateful thoughts are only going to bring you down and also bring your frequency farther away from having what you most desire. Practice this technique as often as possible, paying special attention to the positive feelings you will have when you have what you want.

This chapter has brought your awareness to your mindset, how your thoughts are often programs that are running subconsciously and creating your perception of reality. You have learned that you can change your mindset by becoming aware of your subconscious thoughts. What you are aware of you can change, and this puts creative power back in your hands. You have also become aware that thoughts can get lodged in the body, and I gave you a practice that can help you release those stuck energies, which can clear your body of all sorts of disharmony, discomfort, and dis-ease.

In the next chapter we will dig in deeper and look for the originating program that is likely running your life. When you find it, and excavate the dark seed, your life will change in miraculous ways. Are you ready for an upgrade?

CHAPTER 5:

Excavating the Dark Seed

You have probably heard of "shadow work" and maybe you have done some work on your shadow before. The shadow is the darkness that lives inside of us, the hidden trauma, angst, anger and sadness that runs our dark side from behind the scenes.

Everyone has shadow programming. These are the programs that trigger us and cause us to act out, throw temper tantrums, yell, scream, lament, rant, curse, and stick our middle finger out the window in traffic.

The shadow programs keep us in the past. Past hurt and trauma keep recycling through our bodies and our subconscious memories in order to keep us from repeating the same mistakes, getting in the same traps, and engaging in the same destructive relationships. Well, at least that is what they were designed to do, but they actually don't work well for much or any of that. What often ends up happening is that we *do* get involved in repeating the same destructive patterns and we get triggered by our shadow and we get angry that we made the same mistake or got involved with the same type of relationship again and again. The shadow program will keep popping up until it is confronted and released, and replaced with a new program.

The truth is that all shadow programs stem from the deepest pain and darkness that is buried inside the heart and I call that The Dark Seed. The Dark Seed is the core trigger that all other shadow programs are connected to and stem from. It is the root that keeps growing even when you have done extensive shadow work. The problem is that all shadow programs are actually created by The Dark Seed in order to protect it from being discovered. As long as we have something else to focus on, The Dark Seed will be safe and hidden and it will remain in control behind the scenes. While you are pulling your shadow programs out, leaf by leaf The Dark Seed is growing new sprouts and the cycle seems endless. If you can get to the heart of The Dark Seed, you can transform it. This is the finest expression of alchemy, turning The Dark Seed into a rosebud with the potential to bloom and bring beauty into every area of your life.

One day when I was working with a client on her Dark Seed program, I began to draw the Dark Seed and the triggers that sprouted from it. What I ended up with was a drawing of dark sun/spider. It looks like a dark sun and each of the rays is a shadow program coming from the center seed.

It also looks like a spider, which makes me think about arachnophobia, and how the fear of spiders is a matrix code that reminds us of The Dark Seed. Think about spiders, their fangs, venom, sticky webs where they entrap their prey, and how arachnophobia is so pervasive worldwide. The spiders are showing us where we need to go to work, and how easily we get trapped in our own Dark Seed's web. Our outer world reflects to us what we need to work on internally.

So, how is the Dark Seed affecting you and what can you do about it?

Every time you get triggered, there is an opportunity to notice what is happening. I consider this a gift worthy of celebration! When you are courageous enough to diligently notice your triggers, you have the power to find and alchemize the Dark Seed within you.

Step one is noticing. You can't work with something you don't know is there. When you realize you are triggered and take note of it, you have something to work with.

Each time you find one, you take it from the realm of the unknown into the realm of the known.

Now you can work with it, so this is a great reason to celebrate your success! Celebrate every time you catch yourself being triggered! If you do this successfully, you will look insane to anyone watching. Example: externally, you can be seen screaming profanities and flipping off the driver who cut you off in traffic, immediately followed by smiling, laughing, and clapping for yourself. The person in your passenger's seat is going to be concerned.

But internally, it goes something like this: "Aaaaah! I can't believe these freakin' drivers, what a jerk cutting in front of me like that!" You flip off the driver who cut you off, your body is hot, your anger is surging, you feel like you are going to explode, and your face is turning red. Then you realize you are having a reaction, you are triggered, and you have caught yourself. You are suddenly observing the absurdity of your behavior as if for the first time. It looks ridiculous. Have you never pulled in front of someone in traffic before? Of course you have. And it wasn't a personal attack on the driver behind you. You realize how silly it is for you to behave like a toddler, and you celebrate your realization by laughing and applauding.

Step two is recording or writing it down. This is where you pick up your phone and record what just happened (don't do this while driving). For one week, I want you to keep a journal or record a note on your phone every time you experience an upset. It doesn't matter how small it is, it is your job to notice and record even the smallest upset or feeling of victimization. Keep recording your trigger experiences. Sometimes, you won't be able to celebrate right away, sometimes it will take a while to cool down and reflect. But you are on to something *big*. You are excavating the rays of the dark sun, you are digging for gold, and if you keep recognizing and recording your triggers, you will have a roadmap to the treasure chest – The Dark Seed which you will then be able to transform.

Step three is drawing the map. Draw a black circle in the center of a blank sheet of paper. Draw lines going out from the center, just like you drew the sun when you were a child. Leave enough room to write on each line. Now, go over your notes from the week. For each experience that triggered you, write down a few words to summarize the trigger. For instance, getting triggered in the traffic scenario could be, "Driver cutting in front of me." Maybe you got triggered at work when someone took credit for an idea that you had first. Your phrase could be a "stolen idea." Maybe someone snuck in front of you in the checkout line at the grocery store. That one could be "line budger." If someone was late to meet you and you felt upset by it, you could write "made me wait."

Place the phrases on the lines coming out of the circle on your page. The visual and physical act of doing this exercise can add a lot of clarity that is hard to get to when you are just doing it mentally.

Step four is naming the Dark Seed. To do this, write all of your phrases out and see if you can find the common thread. These are clues to piercing the heart of your Dark Seed. There is always a theme, even if it seems to be hidden. Work with it and see if you can find the theme of your Dark Seed.

In the example above, the theme is disrespect. The driver "cut you off," and you felt unseen, unnoticed, and discounted. Someone cut in front of you in line and the same feeling of not being important emerged. The idea was stolen without giving you proper credit and you were not feeling honored or respected.

This part requires leaning into the feelings that are triggered when you have the emotional upset. Really dive into what you are feeling in the trigger. This requires emotional maturity. You must extract yourself from blaming and victimization and observe what is really going on.

The idea here is to discover what is running you. There is a negative program that you have to find in order to reprogram it. Keep looking for it. When you find it, you will know. Your body will have a reaction of some sort. You will feel it. Write it down. You may have more than one, and that is fine too. Write down everything you discover about your shadow programming.

If you had to pick one word to label the Dark Seed what would it be? Mine was rejection. My theme was being left, left out, and left behind. It always led to a feeling of being unwanted or rejected.

Was it true? Well, those things really did happen, but was it *true?* No. I perceived what happened as rejection, but rejection is not the truth. Rejection was the filter that was casting a veil on various experiences I was having. It was like wearing colored lenses; the lenses were the color of rejection, so I saw and felt rejected. When I was able to realize that rejection was just a program I was running, and I could transform it by removing the lenses. Those same situations will continue to happen but I no longer experience rejection. That is a relief.

Was it painful to dig in and excavate the Dark Seed of rejection? Yes! Was it worth it? Yes, beyond my wildest dreams! To be free of the heaviness and baggage of a lifetime of feeling rejected feels as if my entire world became lighter, more peaceful, and more beautiful. The rose is blooming where the rotting compost used to be.

So, step one is noticing, step two is recording or writing it down, step three is drawing the map, step four is naming the Dark Seed, and the final step is alchemy. It's time to turn the Dark Seed into gold, the compost into the rose.

The Original Separation

Whatever your Dark Seed label turns out to be, I believe that all of our triggers, upsets, and feelings of disrespect and rejection can be traced back to a single origin. The original fall, the choice we made to separate from oneness into form. In the beginning, we were light. We were one with Source, there was no knowledge of being anything other than the divinity that we are.

That *I am*, because before the original separation, there was only one; there was no *we*, there was only *I*. I wanted to expand and experience more. I separated into form and became we. The memory of oneness never fully left the heart. This is the longing, the yearning, the deep desire for connection. This internal remembrance of being *all as one* is still very much alive in the heart.

As a meditation teacher, a breathwork practitioner, and a Lucia Light practitioner, this is what every one of my clients is looking for – a connection to something greater, the return to Source, the yearning to be alleviated. It is embedded in the fabric of our existence. We desire to feel connected. The thing that has us hide from that is our fear of rejection and our misunderstanding of the original separation from oneness. The experience of self-doubt, self-loathing, of not being good enough doesn't begin with childhood or a past life, or your starseed planet sending you to a mission on Earth. It goes farther back than that to Source desiring to expand and know itself, which required separation. But the separation was always for the purpose of expansion, not because you weren't good enough. That program got distorted along the way. I am divine, you are divine, we have always been and always will be divine. We chose this experience to grow, to learn, to expand, to play, to feel, to experience life in all of its glory. Experience the sadness, the lack, fear, anger, and negativity, and even the dark night of the soul. Because when we fall, we get back up, and from there we expand and we grow into the remembrance of the luminescence that we truly are. The compost is nourishment for the soul to bloom in. This is how the Dark Seed becomes the blooming rose.

Now you are familiar with the Dark Seed concept, that your behavior and triggers come from a deep place within you, and that once recognized, this shadow program can be identified, labeled and ultimately released. The next chapter will get into specific ways to transform the Dark Seed programming and all programming that stems from it. The RHOS technique of recoding will allow you to transform any program you find running you, as well as upgrading your body and your perception of the life you are living. You will have the ticket of transformation in your pocket, and with it, you can change everything.

CHAPTER 6:

The Alchemy of Recoding

In the last chapter, you learned about the Dark Seed and how it's shadow programming can sabotage your reality, casting a veil of negativity over your experiences. When you become diligent with recognizing your triggers and working with them, your triggers no longer have power over you. You become free of the heaviness that was weighing you down. You are less reactive and more centered, balanced, and clear.

Now comes the fun part: the recoding. This is how we alchemize our triggers into gold. The Dark Seed begins as your kryptonite, the thing that takes you down in a flash, but with recoding, the Dark Seed is alchemized into your superpower! The thing that once created the most frustration and upset in your life can now be the seed of contentment.

RHOS (Recoding the Human Operating System)

RHOS is the technical manual for reprogramming your body, mind, and spirit from being triggered by the things that daily life throws at you to being centered in your knowledge that you are whole and complete and you are the master of your life. This process came to me in a meditation one day. I was on a two-month tour, and at the time, I was in my very first location, the beginning of a journey that would change my life dramatically. I was in Puebla, Mexico staying at a comfortable and quaint Airbnb. I woke up and went straight into my morning meditation, as I usually do. In my meditation, I began to see the big picture, the way that recoding can be used in the body to lose weight, regenerate, and become younger, recoding for youth, energy, vitality, health, my vision, and loneliness. Recoding the Human Operating System! At that moment, it seemed like an instant download from the Divine, but actually, I've been working on this for thirty years and that was the magical moment that all of the pieces came together.

The Download

I saw the "cocoon" I was placed in by the "visitors" when I was a child. It was a recoding station, downloading my body and my energy field with the programs I would need to complete the mission I came here for. I saw my sword as a USB drive that can be used to reprogram, recode myself and others. I saw my diamond light crown and robe, sparkling and shimmering in etheric starlight energy – the energy of this new code! I understood that *I am* the code, waiting to activate to greater frequencies and higher dimensional realities. I saw all of my lifetimes in my multidimensional awareness that I have lived, or am currently living in another realm, because time is a third dimensional construct, and everything is happening now. I saw myself as an Egyptian priestess in the Temple of Isis and I saw how I was activated, initiated into the embodiment of the Divine. I saw myself as Lemurian light codes in the water, moving as light and carrying codes to inform, activate, and upgrade all of the beings of the water, including the crystal cities within the water dimensions and that I could travel through portals to my home star of Sirius, B, or to the Pleiades, or to any star that had information for me to deliver, and I would "download" the information and take it where it was needed. I did that for eons of time, a multidimensional light code currier traveling through portals of time and space. I could upgrade a whole species by downloading new codes into their DNA. I saw myself as a feline being in a light ship guarding and holding the frequency of the frequency generator that powered all of the pyramids in "ancient" Egypt, which is more accurately future Egypt, but as I said, multidimensionally all is happening now, so there is no past or future, there is only now.

I also saw scenes from my current life where I gave away or lost my power, and I understood that I must immediately retrieve the power I lost in those experiences.

I did a soul retrieval for myself at that moment. I activated my New Template, the crystalline blueprint and brought myself fully back "online". I understood then that I am an Architect of the New Code. My mission and service is to Recode the Multidimensional Human Operating System. I am the Light Codes still, here in this human body, I am all of my incarnations and I can channel all of my multidimensional self.

I received the command from Source: "You have the template; now embody it. The template exists on a slightly higher timeline. When you embody it you move to the new timeline. Use language to transmit the new code. Invite, but do not attempt to convince. Lead with love. Love breaks down resistance. Always lead through the heart."

This began a series of transmissions, upgrades, and embodiment of Source that continued and escalated throughout my two-month tour. My next stop was Valle Del Bravo, where my diamond heart was activated when I was guided in meditation into the city of Telos under Mount Shasta. Here is where I met Adama, the High Priest of Telos. Ascended Sananda accompanied me there and the two of them, Sananda and Adama reconnected me with my twin flame, who I was told I would reunite within Mount Shasta, where I would be going toward the end of my tour.

During this visit, I was receiving download after download of spiritual technologies that I would be using in my Ascension Training work. The goddess Isis began working with me more directly in my meditations. I had been working with Isis for as long as I could remember, but now she was ever-present with me and serving as my guide in this new awakening and embodiment of my activated crystalline body.

The Human Tech

I refer to the body as the "Human Operating System." This is how I received it from Source, and the reason is so that we can wrap our minds around the body as a very sophisticated technology that we have been gifted with at birth here on planet Earth. It is like starting a new job with a top of the line mobile computer that is ready to instantly download programs from every interaction, person, place, and situation. It comes pre-programmed with an unimaginable amount of information already, but for most humans, most of that information is not accessible until much

THE LOVE YOU CRAVE

later, and then it will only be accessible in special circumstances, through spiritual work, meditation, activations, or near-death experience. The majority of people will probably not access their multidimensional memories, but the memories are there, latent, just waiting to be accessed for those who are courageous and willing to do the work.

The body, as I have mentioned before, stores every thought, feeling, emotion, and every memory of all of our life experiences. This doesn't mean that we remember or experience the "truth," however, because what we experience is always a projection of our inner belief system. Our reality is projected through the veil of our thoughts and beliefs, and our body feels emotion according to our thoughts, beliefs, and perception of what is happening in the world around us.

The body can be programmed for negativity or positivity, or to have no reaction at all. The mind recycles thoughts from the past, rehearsing what it believes will keep us alive (it's worked this long, so it's doing its job!), and our spirit has the job of choosing our behavior, making conscious decisions and thoughts, and it is the spirit's job to manage and master the human technology. This is a big job, and if you have a lazy spirit you may just be running on autopilot. But if you choose to master your human tech, you can become the master of this reality, and this is where the real excitement, creativity, and fun is, for those who

58

are courageous enough to do the work and become the master.

Are you ready?

The RHOS Process

You began the last chapter with writing down what triggered you for a week, so you have your triggers and your Dark Seed has a label (such as "rejection.")

Now, it is time to choose a "recode" word. You are going to find a word that alleviates the heaviness that you feel from your Dark Seed. I chose to start with "effervescence." Effervescence is the bubbly, tingly feeling of lightness, like bubbles in champagne, and I like the visual of the bubbles breaking up the shadow program. The recode word does not need to be the opposite of your trigger, although if it feels right you can play around with possibilities. The important thing to remember is that your recode word should not be too extreme, because you can't usually go from feeling rejection to feeling loved, or from feeling angry to feeling joy.

But you may be able to go from feeling disrespected to feeling refreshed. It helps to have a visual with your recode word, like the bubbles in effervescence. You could imagine an ocean breeze with the word "freshness" or a ray of sun for "lightness," or you could visualize the smoke of burning sage with a recode word of "smudge" or "clearing." Play with words and find something that feels right to you. You can change the words as you go so pick one now and if it isn't working for you it's ok to choose a new one later.

For the next week, every time you notice yourself getting triggered, no matter how mundane or small it seems, you will be using your recode word to upgrade your experience.

Remember, first you must recognize that you are feeling triggered. This can be subtle or extreme but celebrate that you noticed. Catching yourself being triggered is half the battle!

Once you are aware of feeling triggered this is the beginner's guide to RHOS:

1. Notice what triggered you
2. Notice how you feel emotionally as a result of the trigger
3. Where in your body are you feeling it?

Don't hide from the emotion and the physical experience. Really notice it and allow yourself to feel it.

1. Now, amplify the feeling in your body times ten, then times 100. Make it so strong that your body can't hold it anymore. Then blast the feeling with light, like a meteor of white light blasting into your body and release the feeling into the blast of light.

2. Bring in your code word. Speak your code word into the area of your body where you released the trigger from. Speak it out loud three times or more.

3. Hum a tone into the place in your body that you are recoding. You don't have to be a singer and it doesn't matter how it sounds, just use your humming voice to fill the space and empower the frequency of your code word. Feel the vibration of the hum... this is frequency healing. As you hum, imagine that the new code you are programming yourself with is growing stronger and stronger. It is completely overriding the old program. Keep humming until you feel filled with the new code and wrap your body in white light to hold the frequency.

Congratulations, you have just completed your first round of recoding. Your body is now learning to hold a new frequency, and this is an integral step in your ascension process.

Do this every time you get triggered. If you are in public, go somewhere as soon as possible, even if it's the restroom, and do this. It doesn't matter if other people hear you, your new reality is way more important than what they think.

As you get comfortable and confident with your recoding process, you can upgrade your code words. As you become masterful you can try going from comfort to joy, from lightness to enlightened, or from refreshed to ecstatic! Play with the codes and have fun with the words. Make it a game for yourself, and your reward for winning will be a higher frequency, a feeling of lightness, and emotional clarity.

You can use this process to reprogram pain in your body. Do everything the same, but rather than waiting for a trigger, focus on the part of your body where you feel pain and work with it.

You can also reprogram traumatic memories. Remember that the memories you hold are not the *truth*, but rather the perceived experience you had, and they are not fixed, they are malleable, moldable, changeable. Working with traumatic memories can be difficult but extremely rewarding. When you reprogram the trauma in your body, you allow it to release and you replace it with a higher frequency memory, emotion, or idea. Work with recoding your memories and you will begin to release yourself from the heaviness that you didn't know you were carrying. My clients consistently report feeling "lighter," "peaceful," and "happier" from doing this work. You can do this for your pain, your disease, your weight, your belly fat, diet, exercise, anything you want to recode in your body or your life.

There is a RHOS meditation included with the website materials.

This is a version of the RHOS meditation that you can read, practice, have someone read it to you, or even record in your own voice and listen to it as a guided meditation.

Drop into your heart center. Remember, you must focus from your heart center in order to do this work.

Feel the trigger there. Notice what happens to your body – sensations, etcetera.

Notice *where* you feel it in your body – certain areas or organs?

Ask your body if it is willing to surrender the pain associated with this trigger.

Wait for your body to respond.

When you feel a *yes* from your body, thank it.

If your body won't agree to surrender, encourage it to allow this process.

Once the body aligns, call up your recode word.

Speak your code word into the trigger, into the upset, into the place in your body, into the organ(s) associated. Feel the loosening of the congested energy.

Feel the feeling of the recode – how is it changing the experience?

Ask your body to release the upset into the frequency of the new code.

How does the new code feel in your body?

Can you get a sense of the energy dissipating?

Speak the recode into the body again, into the energy of the upset.

Call in the Platinum flame.

Tune in to the transformational power of the platinum flame and use the flame to burn off the old code, to burn off the feeling of the trigger, and to purify your body internally and externally of the old trigger code. This is transformational *alchemy*.

Again, use the new code word to reprogram, re-inform your body.

Feel the release, the opening, and the lighten-ing within and around the space where the old code was hiding.

You are alchemizing the coal into diamond light within you – crystalizing the trigger to transform into positive creative energy.

Feel the frequency of the new code as it fills you internally, informing your organs, muscles, blood-stream, cells, and your DNA.

Feel the lightness of the new code within and around you.

Remember this feeling.

Next time you do this it will be easier, stronger, and faster.

You are now attuned to the new code.

CHAPTER 7:

From Resistance to Surrender

Resistance is the thing that keeps us from everything we've ever wanted. It shows up as procrastination, self-doubt, hunger, sickness, distraction, lack of focus, back pain, the dog needing a walk, the kids wanting your attention, guilt, fear, anger, and melancholy. And that's just the beginning.

Resistance is the frequency, the code of not doing, not having, not completing, waiting until...you get the idea. It is the ego resisting change.

The reason you don't have your ideal partner, your master's degree, your best life, whatever that is for you is that you succumb to resistance. Not just once, but often, daily, possibly hundreds of times a day. Resistance is a strong program. It keeps us locked in the box. When we start to poke around and look for potential ways out of the box, resistance has a bottomless bag of tricks to keep us right where we are. Change is dangerous in the ego's mind. The ego's job is to keep you safe. If it could speak it would say, "Just keep doing what you did yesterday and everything will be fine." But you and I both know it won't be fine. It will be the same. The same boring life that you have been living, *not* living out your wildest dreams, *not* enjoying every minute, *not* experiencing your greatest purpose and *not* inspiring the world with your boldness and creativity. Consequently, when you leave this world if you spent your life under the stronghold of resistance, what will you be remembered for? In ten years? In one hundred?

Resistance keeps you playing small, but you were designed for more. You have dreams, ideas, goals, and you are here to make a difference. You have a purpose and the world is waiting! This is your life, you only live this life once and now is your moment to really *live*, so let's take this resistance and kick it to the curb!

Surrender is the state of releasing resistance. Giving in to your higher calling, listening to the call of the Divine, and allowing yourself to go deeper, farther, to take the risk, to have courage in the face of fear. Surrender leads to communion with the Divine. The biggest hurdle I have encountered in my spiritual path is learning to surrender and surrender more and surrender more. When I have arrived at a point where

I felt that if I surrender any more I would be losing my life, and I still chose to surrender, *that* is where I've had the greatest growth spiritually. If you have had this experience, you know what I mean, but if you haven't, it is probably hard to grasp.

You must be compliant to the higher source energy in order to grow spiritually. The scriptures say you are most moldable when you are in the *fire*. The *fire* is where we give up resistance. It is intense, the stakes are high, life and death, no room for questioning. The fire is when we are confronted with life's most difficult times. Trauma leads to compliance, compliance creates flexibility, and flexibility is moldable.

You can use the fire to create flexibility and mold yourself into who you want to be. You don't have to wait for difficulty or trauma to become moldable, to enter the fire. The fire of spirit is always burning, and ready to guide you into flexibility.

I imagine you have had one or more traumatic experiences where you were consumed by the fire and became moldable, compliant, and maybe you experienced an epiphany at that moment. But you do not have to experience trauma to have transformation. You can learn to surrender without the trauma.

When I was attending a meditation seminar years ago, my meditations were consistently leading me into shamanic style journeys where I would be confronted with death. This was a five-day retreat and I had just moved to Florida and I was concerned with alligators. I had grown up in Iowa, and I'd never lived in proximity to potential predators, so it was on my mind. In this meditation, I found myself in the water with a large and hungry alligator. At that point, I could have gone into resistance and come out of my meditation as if waking up from a nightmare. But I had done too much work to get there, and I remembered Dr. Joe saying, "Whatever shows up, lean into it, let it take you deeper." I did. At that moment, I chose to surrender to the alligator. I decided to allow the experience and see what would happen. If you are not familiar with this style of journeying meditation, the experience is very real. There is an aspect of mind that knows this is a trance, a deep meditative state, kind of like a dream state, and somewhat like a lucid dream, but this is a meditative journey and most of the consciousness is deeply involved with what is being experienced in the journey. At times, it can feel and seem *more real* than the regular waking state.

The alligator consumed me. It grabbed me, dragged me to the bottom of the water, strangled me, and consumed me. I didn't resist; I had decided to just go with the experience and observe it all in compliant curiosity, so instead of a horribly unpleasant experience, I found myself thinking, "Woah, what's this, what is he doing now? This is interesting, yep, he's going to eat me... I wonder what this will be like..."

I didn't experience any pain because the pain comes from resistance and where there is no resistance, there is no pain. The next thing that happened was the alligator excreted me. I became fertile ground for a lotus seed, and the next thing I experienced was being the lotus flower. I grew up from a root at the bottom of the river, I became a flower bud, and I felt the glorious warmth and nourishment of the sunlight. I burst open, opening my petals to the sun, and I felt more alive than I had ever felt before, more joy, more openness, more love and vitality. I was transformed!

I released my fear of alligators in that meditation, I surrendered fear of death, and I was so grateful to have experienced the Lotus, *what a blessing* that surrender had turned into!

That entire seminar was filled with similar meditations, the experience of falling to my (body's) death only to find myself flying through the cosmos, being blown up and into a much more beautiful place than I ever could have imagined, drowning, exploding, burning, being consumed by predators, and every time, it led my consciousness to transform into something more incredible, blissful, fulfilling, and expansive than before. I learned to surrender to Divine will, and that the greatest glory comes from letting go.

In my final meditation of that seminar, I found myself suspended in a luminous pink crystal cave. The crystals were gigantic, each point being much larger than my body. I was immobile and I looked around to see what was holding me in this state of suspension. It appeared to be a sticky web. "Oh boy," I thought, "it's a spider web... a gigantic, sticky, crystalline spider web. If there is a spider web, there must be a spider."

Yes, I have a fear of spiders, and naturally, my subconscious would bring out this deep-seated fear for the final meditation of the seminar. I wasn't afraid as I looked around. The scenery was thrilling and the frequency those enormous pink crystals were giving off was filling my entire body with tingling, electric energy. I attempted to look behind me, and there I could see, in my peripheral vision, a giant spider, many times larger than myself, and it had massive pink crystal fangs. The spider itself looked to be crystalline in structure, it was looking right at me with its multiple eyes, and I knew it was "time." I sent a thought to the luminous crystalline monster, "If you are going to bite me, could you do it here?" I gestured to my lower back. "I have been sitting in meditation all week and I am ready to alchemize this back pain!" At that point, I was excited for the spider to bite me because I knew my back pain would be transformed and released with the powerful venom of this magnificent arachnid. It was at that very moment, as the spider approached me, that Dr. Joe started speaking. "Now... return your consciousness to the present..."

I was transported back to my present awareness of meditating in a ballroom with 1,000 other students. I didn't get to experience the spider's venom, and I was *disappointed!* What a turnaround. After that meditation retreat, I have almost no fear of spiders, alligators, or any other predator. My fear of death is so diminished. I have a healthy respect for my body and preserving it, of course. I respect all creatures that could end the life of my body and I wouldn't put myself in harm's way. But I don't fear them now; I appreciate them. This is one of the superpowers of surrender... it can turn fear into respect, appreciation, even love.

When you find yourself trying to focus or meditate, but your mind keeps taking you out with random thoughts, take a deep breath and ask yourself, "How can I surrender more?"

Breathe deeply into your belly and listen. There is inevitably something within you holding you back. Some thought, feeling, belief, or old program is trying to distract you from realizing your potential. Let it speak. Give it a voice. This is the inner voice of your Dark Seed and it will speak to you when you create a safe place for it. Remember, it's not bad, and it holds the key to everything in your life that has kept you from realizing your potential, your dreams, it holds the key to freeing you from fear. Respect it and listen to what it has to say. Surrender to it the way I did to the alligator and the spider, and see what it will show you.

When you break through the fear of the darkness and respect its power when you lift the veil that you have been hiding behind and you walk right into the heart of your deepest fear... you will find freedom. You will see that what you fear, even if it's fear of death, holds no power over you. You have been feeding it your fear all of this time, and you believed it would destroy you, and maybe it nearly did. But not any-more. Now, with your new superpower of surrender, you can become the Dark Seed's ally. You can befriend it, look it in the eye, and sit down for a heart-to-heart. You can listen to it and hear it's voice telling you why it has done all of the evil things it has put you through. You can see now that it has always been your ally, pushing you toward change, amplifying that which you were most afraid of in order to get you to move, do something different, break out of your old habits and boxes, and shake you up so that you would get into the fire. The fire of transformation, where you become moldable and pliable, where you release your resistance to change and where you dig deep inside yourself and find out that you are *divine!*

You don't have to get hit by lightning or have a dark night of the soul to start listening to your inner darkness. You can do it right now, wherever you are, whatever point you are in in your life. You are never too young, old, rich, poor, healthy or unhealthy to open up to the wisdom of your inner truth. This is the whole point of your being here now. There has never been a better time and there will never be a better time than now. Now is all you have. So, I encourage you to do it now. Surrender to your divine truth. Go deep, surrender more, go deeper, and surrender more. Whenever you hit a "wall" and don't think you can go any further, surrender more. If you are arguing with your partner, family member, friend, coworker, or yourself, surrender. Keep releasing your resistance. You are only fighting yourself. When you can surrender to what is, there is nothing left to fight. This is where peace and happiness emerge.

Remember that the original separation is the separation from oneness, from God, from the purity of the Divine. The core of darkness stems from the unworthiness we inevitably feel from what seems like being unworthy of God, being rejected from heaven, banished from wholeness. You are the wholeness. You chose to separate, to learn, to grow, to expand, to feel. And ultimately, to surrender. Now it is time to surrender your unworthiness and accept your wholeness, your power, your completeness. When you stand in your completeness, when you release your belief/program that you are inherently unworthy, you don't need anything from anyone else. In this place, you can have relationships based on your wholeness. You don't engage with anyone else from your need, or your fear, but you engage from your sense of wholeness. This is the foundation of a strong relationship. Commit to yourself first. Commit to love yourself. Surrender your unworthiness. Reprogram it to wellness, completeness, and an abundance of love. From there, you can engage in unconditionally loving relationships.

Allow more- more light, more truth, more money, more love.

You can use the surrender process for any area you want to allow more in your life. If you want spiritual expansion, tune in and ask yourself "What do I need to surrender in order to open up to my spiritual gifts?" or "What do I need to release in order to experience a deeper connection to the divine?"

Here are some good questions to ask yourself in a situation where you can't find an answer:

- "What is in the way of my experiencing deeper truth, deeper understanding?"
- "What is in the way of me seeing the answer, what do I need to surrender to see what is really going on?"
- "What obstacle is in the way of my knowingness?"
- "What do I need to release?"
- "How can I release more?"

Ask yourself questions like these in order to allow more prosperity in your business, career, job, etcetera:

- "Where am I blocking myself in receiving? How can I release my blocks to receiving"?
- "Where am I closed off to new opportunities? What do I need to surrender to allow new opportunities into my life?"

And finally, ask yourself these about love:

- "How am I blocking myself from love? How can I surrender to love more?"
- "What do I need to release in order to allow myself to love... to be loved?"

You can use this internal line of questioning for any block or any trait you want to develop. Become generous in your listening. Learn to understand the way your human technology communicates with you. Sometimes it is in a feeling, a tingle, a whisper, a vision. Let yourself receive in the way that works for you. Continue to create and open your line of communication with your body, your sacred tech. You will gain confidence in this as you practice. There is no one set way; it is unique to you, so play, experiment, and practice. You are the master programmer of your machine!

Now you are clear that resistance is the thing that stands between you and the life you were born to live, and surrender is the state of releasing resistance. What are you willing to surrender to have your best life? When you have surrendered enough of your resistance something magical begins to happen. You become lighter, the world of energy is more available, life is more playful, and you open to higher frequencies. The next chapter will lead you into the embodiment. This is the good stuff, the wonderful payoff for surrendering your resistance is on its way...are you ready to receive the Divine Frequencies?

CHAPTER 8:

Embodying the Divine Frequencies

Embodiment is defined as "a tangible or visible form of an idea, quality, or feeling."

"she seemed to be a living embodiment of vitality" (google)

The embodiment I'm discussing here is about holding frequencies in your body. You have had moments of feeling good, great, ecstatic, feeling powerful or even invincible. You may have had moments of feeling deep contentment, peace, and even extremely high-frequency feelings such as *the peace that passes understanding*. If you have felt that, you know what I'm talking about, and if you haven't yet, you will!

Embodiment is feeling everything there is to feel in order to get to attune your system to be capable of holding higher frequency feelings. You first must experience and release the lower frequency feelings that you are used to feeling and that you are probably addicted to.

Some of these include drama (the feelings that engaging in drama brings) which is very addictive, anger, sadness, guilt, lack, self-doubt, self-loathing, feelings of being victimized, feelings of separation/loneliness, illness, and pain. Yes, you are probably addicted to one or more of these states and the feelings that you get from engaging in them. How can you tell? Do you go looking for trouble when things are too calm? Do you scroll social media and engage in political posts? Do you start thinking of that friend who betrayed you (weeks ago!), or maybe you get sick- a cold, allergies, or bigger illnesses... all of these are forms of emotional energy taking us away from the embodiment of something higher- our higher truth, higher service, and the divine. We have to clear out the addictions and habitual repetition of engaging in these low frequency emotional and physical states in order to embody the Divine.

This is *not* a Spiritual bypass – you *must feel* with and *in* the body. This is the opposite of Spiritual Bypass, this is bringing *more* awareness, information, and feeling into the body. This is opening and attuning your nervous system to hold higher frequencies.

As children, we may begin being wide open, but at some point, we shut down the nervous system. We learn to tune out what is uncomfortable. We avoid pain; we seek comfort. Sometimes, we have a major shutdown. Traumatic childhood experiences can cause a shutdown, as can any type of sexual trauma at any age.

Empathic children who feel everything can become overwhelmed and stop feeling, even turning off the feeling and emotional centers because it's just too much to feel. I did that.

Then there are shutdowns caused by circuitry overload. This can happen when someone has a near-death experience (NDE), or an instant awakening, downloading so much energy and information at once that it is too much to process, like being hit with a bolt of lightning. In these cases, it is necessary to *reset* the circuit breaker. That requires downtime, quiet time, meditation, integration, and recalibration. Rebooting your emotional and feeling body.

The process of releasing addiction to the old emotions and holding lower frequencies in the body may take some time. Be diligent and work with yourself. Give yourself room to explore your mental and emotional states without judgment. Judging is another low-frequency characteristic. Give up judging yourself and others. Replace judgment with acceptance, and when you are able to accept in non-judgment, you can begin to love.

Lack consciousness (AKA unworthiness) is pervasive. Nearly everyone has it in one form or another. If you have enough money, love, energy, spiritual openness, and enough of everything you desire, then feel free to skip this part. The frequency of lack is held in the body, the mind (in beliefs) and in the energy field. There are layers to every emotional state that you have habitually been running. You will have to address and upgrade each layer before you can attune to holding higher frequencies. Let's take it step-by-step.

1. Get into a contemplative, meditative state.

2. In order to find lack, you first have to get present to the frequency of it. Tune in to the frequency of lack. Think of any part of your life where you feel the void of something you are missing. It may help to focus on one thing, such as love, money, or spiritual connection. Focus on the feeling of *not* having it; how does it feel in your body, what emotions does it bring up, and how do you feel energetically?

3. Now that you know what you are looking for, scan your body, your mind, your memories, and your energy for the experience of lack. Notice where you feel anything that resonates with the frequency of lack,

limitation, not having, needing, wanting, yearning, etc.

4. Trust your body's wisdom to guide you. When you find a place in your body that calls your attention, notice it. Hyper-focus on it. It may begin with a whisper, a tingling, or a small pain, so be diligent in your noticing. It may show up as intense pain, more of a yelling or screaming than a whisper. If so, *great!* You don't have to wonder if you found it; you can be sure. Now, hyper-focus on that area. Or if you have found a memory or an energetic sensation, ask your body where (in what part of your body) does this emotion, memory, or energy reside or relate to? If you find a place, work there. If you can't relate it to the body, that's okay. Just work with whatever you find.

5. Now that you have the frequency and you know the place where you are holding it, go into communication with it. Ask it where it came from and what it is doing there. Note any information you receive. You may be surprised at what it tells you. Let it tell you everything it wants to say. Just take note. Be the non-biased reporter, asking and listening.

6. Now ask your body if it is ready to release this low-frequency thought/belief/energy that it has been holding. Listen for the "Yes." If your body doesn't want to release the energy, remind the body that this energy is no longer serving you and that you are going to replace it with something much better. Continue until you feel the "Yes."

7. Now amplify the feeling of the lack by ten and by 100; amplify it so powerfully that it *must* release and release it from your body. Repeat this if necessary until you feel the release and the relief of letting it go.

8. Great work! Now fill that space with something beautiful. You choose what to put there. If you cleared lack, put in prosperity or an abundance of what you prefer to feel. Love, wholeness, comfort, peace, self-acceptance, forgiveness... it is your choice. Put in what feels right to you. Just make sure it is a positive feeling frequency that is an upgrade to what you have released.

This is a version of RHOS; you are upgrading and recoding through identifying, amplifying, and releasing the old program. You will likely need to do this multiple times. I recommend you do it every day for two weeks or as long as you feel it is necessary to fully reprogram a body of belief, emotion, pain, or energy.

There are ways to amplify the release and embodiment process. Breathwork is a powerful practice that can help you move stuck energy and breakthrough much faster as well as helping you open up and feel the new frequencies you are ready to embody. I am a breathwork teacher and my classes are specifically designed to help you release the old and embody the new programs and frequencies you are working with. You can find a free introductory breathwork class on my website to accompany this book.

Surrendering Resistance and Opening to the Ascended Frequencies

Remember what you just read about surrender in the last chapter? You can use surrender to help you release old pain and trauma. Release resistance. Surrender is a constant as you journey into opening to ascended frequencies.

I have been given some amazing spiritual technologies that can assist the amplification of your manifestation abilities, your ability to release old programs, recode to your new programs, draw empowering frequencies to you, and assist you in creating the life you are here to live. Some of these were handed down to me through my teachers, others came direct in meditation.

I will give you a brief introduction to these technologies here. To learn more about them, to get an attunement to them, or to find out how you can gain personal access and greater proficiency with these frequencies visit waxelasananda.com.

The Golden Rod

A woman woke up inside a dream to find a wizard guide had come to teach her an important lesson. She got up and followed the wizard to the water.

The wizard said, "We are going fishing. Go ahead and catch some fish."

The woman attempted to catch fish, grasping at them in the water, but the fish kept slipping away from her. She looked at the wizard and told him she didn't know how to catch the fish.

"That's not how you do it." He chuckled. "Watch me."

The wizard produced a golden rod which he planted at the sandy bottom of the water where he stood. He stood tall holding the golden rod close to his body and the fish surrounded him in abundance. The woman watched in amazement as the fish filled the wizard's basket to overflowing and he didn't even have to move.

The wizard handed the woman his golden rod.

"Now, you do it!" he commanded. "Hold the rod with both hands, tune into your heart, and call the fish to you."

The woman held the rod, tuned into her heart, and allowed her heart to call the fish. To her amazement, many fish came to her. They kept coming and she could easily fill her basket many times over.

"Now you know how to fish, go and teach the people," the wizard proclaimed.

"But wait..." the woman disputed...

"If I teach the people to do this, it will be too easy to overfish, and the fish population will suffer."

"The people who learn from you will not overfish," assured the wizard, "because in order to use the golden rod, you must first be in your heart. When you request from your heart, you are inviting the fish, and when you fish from your heart, you will only take what you need in balance with life."

The story of the golden rod reminds us that we can receive an abundance of what we desire as long as we request with the heart and receive in balance with life.

I began working with the golden rod immediately after I heard this story and received an attunement to the frequency of the golden rod. I found that every time I went in the water and called forth the golden rod, I would be followed by a number of fish. This is really fun when snorkeling. Of course, the technology of the golden rod is not actually about fish at all, but the fish represent prosperity in whatever form we are ready to receive.

The Diamond Scepter

The next phase of spiritual technology I received was the diamond scepter. After my diamond heart was activated, I began seeing the spiritual diamond technology everywhere. I received the diamond scepter as an instant download in meditation in Valle Del Bravo, Mexico. The diamond scepter looks like a large diamond on top of the golden rod. The diamond amplifies the field coming through the golden rod. It is not solid, but rather the plasmic energy of creation, and it shimmers in reflective brilliance, containing every color of light and creation within it.

The diamond scepter represents the Divine Feminine energy. It is partnered with the Divine Masculine in the golden rod. The diamond is the shape of the womb, and it is the center of creativity. It is activated through the diamond portal in the heart, and a field of intention is sent up from the golden rod, through the diamond scepter, and out around the body. It enters back in through the base of the spine (if you are seated) or through the bottom of the feet if you are standing. You can charge the scepter through your intention. There is a powerful way to use the intention ritual through the diamond scepter technology that creates a magnetic field that can attract anything to you as long as it is attracted through the activated heart and for the highest good. My intention setting process is outlined in the next section, Creation Codes.

You can find activations, attunements, and meditations for using this technology on my website: (link). It is especially useful to use the diamond scepter to help you reprogram the Dark Seed. The amplification the diamond scepter provides will amplify your field assisting you in both releasing what no longer serves you and downloading the new ascension frequencies.

Creation Codes: The Affirmation Process of Intention Setting

This is where you are going to learn what I call the Creation Codes. It is a specific process that will take you from intention setting through birthing your intention. It's not gender specific. We are all creators and we can all birth worlds.

   1. Set your intention

Your intention must be worded in positive language and as if you have already achieved your goal.

For example, if my intention is to become a practicing Kundalini yoga practitioner (even if I don't currently have the time or finances to achieve this goal), I would phrase my intention like this: "I am a certified Kundalini yoga practitioner, leading my community of twenty-five students to a deeper connection with themselves, their breath, and the divine."

2. *See* it (vision)

Now you create an internal vision of yourself as the Kundalini yoga practitioner, leading classes, guiding students, doing the practice in front of the class. Imagine as many details as you can, such as the studio and room where you are teaching, the faces of your students, what you are wearing, the lighting, etcetera. See it all in your internal vision as if it is happening in the present moment, and vision it *from* your own perspective, through your own eyes, not from a bird's eye perspective or an outsider's viewpoint. This is how it would look if you were actually experiencing it first-hand.

3. Feel it

This is very important; you must feel the experience as if it is happening *now*. You must engage with the emotions and the energy you are feeling as the yoga practitioner. Who are you being in that experience? This is the embodiment. Embody yourself as the practitioner. How do you feel about yourself and your accomplishment? The more you feel, the more real it will become, and the more real it becomes the faster you will manifest it. Feel every detail. What is the temperature of the room? What do your clothes feel like on your body? Is your hair up or down, and how does that feel? Are you playing music? What is the music, how does it sound, and how does the music make you feel? The more details you fill in, the more real it becomes. Feel the feels to make it real!

4. Declare it

Now that you can see it and feel it, declare this as your truth! This is where you demonstrate to the Divine that you are *committed* to this vision. This is what you want, and you will do what it takes to create it, receive it, and live it! Amplify this step by signing a declaration statement. Write your intention on the paper and sign your name to it, declaring your commitment to do whatever it takes, regardless of what gets in your way.

5. Claim it

Now you must claim it. Get into a meditative state, close your eyes, focus into your heart center, call up the vision of your intention, call up the feeling of your realized intention, and claim it to be so, out loud and emphatically! In this case, it will sound like this: "I *am* a Kundalini yoga practitioner!" Do this at least five times, becoming more animated and pouring your heartfelt excitement into it, this is you claiming your dream come true!

6. Birth it

Now for the final step: *birth it!* This is doing the action steps necessary to follow through with your claim. In the example of becoming a Kundalini yoga practitioner, you can start by choosing a date that you will complete your training by. Find a training and sign up, even if it is several months in the future, you must put it in your calendar and believe that you are going to do it and start planning for it. You must take action on your claim. Even if it is small steps at a time, those steps will add up. Give yourself a due date and take the action steps necessary to make it happen. Rehearse the other steps daily and combined with the action steps, the Universe will align itself to make this happen with you because you are taking action.

Watch for your resistance, it will come up! Let it, work with it, surrender it. You have the tools to work with any block or obstacle that arises now. Be diligent in confronting your resistance and working the Creation Code steps daily.

Opening to the Ascended Frequencies

You have done your clearing work. You have worked on the Dark Seed, you have confronted your resistance, and you have learned to surrender. You have learned RHOS recoding and how to birth your intentions with the creation code steps.

Now you are ready to open yourself to embody ascended frequencies. This is the really fun part, and it is ongoing. It becomes more and more pleasurable as you practice.

I will demonstrate this through a meditation., however, you can learn to hold the embodiment of these frequencies all of the time, when you are sleeping, awake, meditation, walking, working, driving... all the time, whatever you are doing.

Practicing the embodiment first in meditation, followed by bringing the frequencies into your dream time and the time when you first wake in the morning is the best way to begin.

First, set yourself up.

You can play beautiful, relaxing music on headphones or speakers. Find a comfortable place to sit or lie down, whichever way is most comfortable for you. Make sure you will not be disturbed. Give yourself a minimum of an hour at first, and if you have a day off where you don't have a schedule to follow, even better.

Sink into your comfort, really feeling and enjoying the comfort of just being. Bring to mind every positive thing you think and feel about yourself. This is a time to indulge in self-love, praise, and worthiness, and to generate a feeling of deep well-being.

Honor your body. Scan your body and thank it for serving you. Your body is your ally, your most sacred technology, and you are deepening your trust and communication with it. Thank it, honor it, love it, and open receive its love and gratitude. This is a form of sacred communication, and you are developing the confidence, trust, and compliance of your body to your higher being. Let your body surrender in trust.

Bring up a feeling of gratitude. If you have a hard time doing that on-demand, practice by thinking of a time when you felt most grateful. For me, the time just after the birth of my children always brings the elated emotion I'm looking for.

Practice getting to this deeply open, grateful, and loving emotional state. It's okay if it doesn't happen immediately. The more you practice, the easier it becomes. Call on your heart, open your heart to the Divine, whatever you call the higher Source, open your heart to it and allow it to work with you. You may feel or see celestial or angelic high-frequency beings with you. If it feels right to you, ask them to assist you in your opening. I have found that there are "Ascension guides" who are specifically designed to assist humanity with the raising of our frequency when we invite them. If this concerns you or if you feel the need to protect yourself from lower frequency beings, then set up a bubble of protection for yourself first. I like to set up a golden column of light where I am safe, protected, and connected to all that is. But also know that when you are in a high-frequency state the lower energies can't reach you. You will "outshine" them, and you won't even be accessible to them in your ascended states. I find that any celestial that shows up when I am basking in divine frequencies is always one of love, peace, and service to my Ascension.

When you get to this point, just flow in it. Bask in it as if you are sunbathing, soaking up rays of the sun. Essentially that is exactly what you are doing, you are soaking up Ascension rays, and you are ray-sing your vibration.

Breathe deeply, filling yourself with the pranic energy of the divine light. Feel the Ascension rays flowing through your body, your bloodstream, your cells, and molecules. Let the frequencies upgrade your DNA; you can ask that your DNA be repaired, revitalized, recharged, reprogrammed and that your latent DNA brought back online.

This is a deeply creative state. You can receive healing frequencies, upgrades, spiritual gifts, and many other empowering things can happen while bathing in Ascension frequencies. As you continue to do this process, if it feels right to you, you can begin to receive the Christ Consciousness frequencies. Christ consciousness is the awakened consciousness of your higher self. The embodied divine that you truly are at your highest expression. It is not religious; it is your personal spirituality and it is your awakening process. There is always another layer of surrender, so if you find yourself feeling blocked or unable to feel the higher frequencies, ask your body what it needs to allow more. Just listen and work with yourself. You have the tools. Go deep. Dive into your heart and open more.

Feel the frequencies in every fiber of your body and your being. This is the embodiment. You are training your body to hold higher vibrations and greater love. You are upgrading your nervous system to allow higher frequencies. It is an unfolding layer by layer, and there is always another layer. Listen to the layers and continue to ask yourself what is needed to go deeper. And *feel*.

This is the attunement to Christ Consciousness, which is Ascension.

Ascension is not *up*, it's *in!*

CHAPTER 9:

Entering the Portal of the Heart

The heart is the greatest technology we have. It outperforms any other human tech because we have access to our multidimensional selves through the heart portal. To have an activated heart is to be limitless, multidimensional, to hold access to infinite wisdom, worlds, and timelines. We are no longer bound by the confines of the body. It gives access to all of time, dimension, space, and reality. In the Ascension process, there is no greater asset than the activated heart and knowing how to use it. In this chapter, I will tell you how to activate your heart and how you can use it to expand your experience of life.

There are many ways to activate your heart. We are all unique so what worked for one person may not be your way, but there is a way and it is worth every effort you make to find it.

I will give you many clues and tools here, but it is up to you to take them and do the work.

If you have been practicing the meditations and techniques I've outlined in the previous chapters, you are already well on your way to having an activated heart. Like every other aspect of the human technology, the heart has infinite layers to excavate and it is always possible to open to another level of purity, clarity, and love through doing your heart work.

To begin, you must be willing to forgive yourself and others and to release your resentments. If you are holding on to and carrying trauma in your body, mind, and energy field, you won't gain access to the open heart. Clearing out resentments, trauma, and forgiveness of self and others is a prerequisite.

The heart is a portal of wisdom and consciousness. It is protected from misuse by remaining in a dormant state until you have become a heart-centered being, living life from love and kindness, with compassion for others, the animals, and the earth. Living in a state of loving-kindness is the greatest way to gain access to the wisdom of the heart. Being a heart-centered human is a requirement to receive the key to unlock the heart's beauty. If you only want to unlock the heart for personal gain, it just won't happen.

There is a Hindu legend about a time when all humans were gods, but they abused that divinity. They so abused it that Brahma, the chief god, decided to take it away from them and hide it where they would never find it again.

Where to hide it became the big question. The lesser gods were called into council to consider this question.

: "Where shall we hide humanity's divinity?" The council said, "We will bury humanity's divinity deep in the earth."

But Brahma said, "No, that will not do; one day they will dig down deep into the earth and will find it."

Then they said, "We will sink their divinity into the deepest ocean."

Again Brahma replied, "No, not there, for they will learn to dive into the deepest waters and search the ocean bed and find it."

Then the lesser gods said, "We will take it to the top of the highest mountain and hide it there."

But again, Brahma replied, "No, for eventually humans will climb every high mountain on earth; they will be sure someday to find it and take it up again."

Then the lesser gods gave up and concluded, "We do not know where to hide it, for it seems there is no place on the earth or in the sea that humans will not eventually reach."

Then Brahma said, "Here is what we will do with humanity's divinity. We will hide it deep down in humans themselves; they will never think to look for it there."

Ever since then, the legend concludes, humans have been going to and fro throughout the earth, climbing, digging, diving, exploring, and searching for something already within themselves. The divinity within humanity is still the best-kept secret of the ages.

This demonstrates the search we go on for spiritual awakening. We take courses, read books, go on retreats, and learn everything we can with the mind when the answers are all hidden within the heart. Brahma hid divinity in our hearts, and when we awaken the heart, the divinity within is activated.

The Triangle Portal of the Heart

There is a triangular portal of the heart. It is composed of the unity of the divine masculine, the divine feminine, and the creative energy within the heart itself. When this trinity is implemented and activated, the triangular heart portal awakens and it is now a doorway, a portal to the infinite inner multiverse. This portal is activated when you practice loving-kindness and begin working with the tringle portal. You can visualize it and explore it in meditation.

Find the **Diamond Portal of the Heart** meditation in the website materials.

The Diamond Portal of the Heart

Equally fascinating is the diamond heart technology. The diamond heart can be activated through asking your higher self to activate it, or by having a facilitator guide you in a meditative journey to activate your heart. Like the diamond Scepter, I see the diamond portal in the heart as a liquid crystal sparkling plasmic stargate. It is not hard like an earth diamond, it is made of creative energy itself, and it contains infinite facets. The facets on the diamond contain every possible color, most of the colors are outside the range of vision of our human eyes, but many people report seeing colors within the diamond portal of the heart that do not exist in 3D or even 5D reality. You can travel within the facets into colored rooms which become portals, stargates, or wormholes to other timelines, other dimensions of reality, and sometimes other worlds. You can travel within and through these portals to gain access to a future upgraded version of yourself and beam the energy and frequency of your future self-back to the current reality you are in, causing an instant energetic upgrade. You can use this technique to overcome illness, pain, and limiting beliefs. You can also beam energy into your past, to clear childhood trauma, to rewrite and upgrade your past, and to revise your relationships. The possibilities are unlimited, be creative and play with it. The idea is to gain access to a more empowered, more loving, expanded version of yourself, to embody the new version of yourself, and to use your new energy for good in this life. Yes, you can also use it to create more prosperity. You can then use this new prosperity to serve your truth, your mission, and your purpose generously here and now. Remember to do the action steps necessary to live into this upgraded version of you. Receiving the upgrade is one part of the process, and taking inspired action is another part. You may be struck with new ideas, inspirations, opportunities, and the like, and you must follow through with action if you want to create real change.

Spiritual Gifts: How to Activate Your Divine Gifts through the Heart Portal

As you gain confidence in traveling into the rooms, colors, and dimensions of the heart, you can choose to travel to a time and place where your spiritual gifts are activated. You can choose which gifts are active, or you can ask your heart to guide you to a time and place where you can see yourself in your authentic power with full access to your spiritual gifts. You can see, feel, or get a sense of what your gifts are in this place, and feel the frequency of who you were being as the one with these gifts activated. Beam the activation back to your current self and memorize the frequency of yourself in your empowered vision. It is the same for any trait or situation you want to manifest. See yourself in the vision, feel who you are and how it feels, and memorize the feeling frequency. Then embody the frequency when you return through the portal. Practice with this and you will gain confidence. Remember to take the necessary action steps as you receive guidance and inspiration.

Opening to Your Purpose through the Heart Portal

If you are still unsure of your purpose, you can use the diamond heart portal to find and understand your purpose, your service, and your mission. Use the creation codes of intention from the embodiment chapter. In this case, your intention will be to know your purpose. Bring your intention through the golden triangle portal, into the diamond portal of the heart. Travel into the facet that contains your purpose, where you can see it, feel it, declare it, claim it, and birth it right back into this reality.

Experiencing a Heart Orgasm

I think the perfect note to end this chapter on is the heart orgasm. Yes, it is a real thing, and yes, I have experienced one. I had no idea that it was going to happen to me, and while I had heard of it, I wasn't expecting to experience it myself. I was in a Dr. Joe Dispenza advanced week-long retreat in Cancun, Mexico. My meditations were profound, deep, and blissfully powerful. I felt connected to life, to love, to the mystic, my heart was open, and I had surrendered all resistance. It was during a breathwork session that the energy in my chest began to expand. I was giving myself fully to the breathwork, following Dr. Joe's guidance, and really going for it, whatever "it" was. I was unattached to any outcome and very present in the now. With each round of breathing, I felt the energy in my heart expanding out, the pressure was building, and I was beginning to shake. It was starting to feel really strange. I had done enough breathing and meditation to know that when things start feeling really weird, to lean into it because that's when the real breakthrough happens. I did lean into it, I kept feeling the expansion in my chest building and building until I was sure it would blow up, and then *"bam"* it exploded, and I was in spiritual ecstasy. Floating with the Divine, God, the Universe, Singularity. For that moment I ceased to exist in any form but blissful love. My heart was consumed in undulating waves of love. I have no idea what my body was doing. I may have passed out. I don't have a concept of how long the actual lasted, but the impact of that experience is still with me, and it always will be. It has influenced nearly every decision I have made since it happened. My heart was changed in that experience. It was so much more than a heart orgasm, it was the alchemy of my old, partially open heart to my activated, ascended, open diamond heart. Everything I felt became amplified. I knew from that moment on that I had to live a bigger life, a different life, a more open, expanded, generous, visible, loving life. From that moment on, everything in my life changed.

CHAPTER 10:

Twin Flame Integration

"Your task is not to seek for love, but merely to seek and find all the barriers within yourself that you have built against it."
— Rumi

There is no greater angst than the yearning for love. Desire to love and be loved is embedded within the core of our creation; it is what we build our personalities around, starting in infancy, and it is also what we build our barriers against, after feeling the pain of the loss of love. For many, it is the most unbearable pain, and we go to great lengths to guard against the suffering of a broken heart.

In this exploration, I have realized that I am a "serial monogamist," meaning I have almost always had a primary relationship. I left relatively minimal space between relationships, and sometimes, I would leave one primary relationship for another that I had already decided to engage in. I am also, by definition, an introvert. That doesn't mean I don't like being with people. I do. What it means is that I regain my energy when I am alone. Alone time is essential for my well-being. I'm also a parent. Being in a relationship and also being a parent doesn't provide a lot of alone time, so I found myself always trying to carve out alone time within the context of my life, work, relationships, social life, and parenting. Alone time can be a big challenge. It has caused me to push away friendships and love relationships with people that I find too needy. Convexly, this pattern has often led me to spend too much time alone or *feeling lonely* inside of my relationships.

I have now realized that it is much lonelier feeling alone within the context of a primary relationship than it is to be single. It has been a journey to get here, and I can confidently say now that I am equally happy alone or in a relationship because I realize that my happiness is generated from within myself, and I can be happy with or without other people, with or without a lover, at home or going out with friends. I am grateful for all of my relationships, and I don't *need* them. I engage because I want to and I enjoy being with others, not from a place of trying to fill a void within myself.

How is this possible for someone like myself who has always felt the need to have a love relationship? It is possible because I have integrated my twin flame. I have gone through the fire of deep loneliness and yearning for love (many times) and I have transformed that pain into a deep-seated calm. Now, in the place where I used to feel empty, I feel peace. It is not a fleeting peace, but a peace rooted in heaven and earth, and the center of creation itself. *I am* peace. *I am* whole. No one else can complete me because *I am* complete. The feeling that comes from this completeness is joyful contentment.

I noticed the other day, as I was chatting with a friend on the phone, that I was able to listen to an upset that she was sharing with me, and while I was empathizing with her, holding space for her to express her pain, I maintained my center of peace, calm, and happiness. It was the first time I became consciously aware that I could simultaneously listen with compassion to the pain of another, be a safe place for that person to share their pain, and also hold my vibration of calm, peace, love, and happiness. For a moment, I felt a layer of my consciousness observing myself and wondering, is it really okay to listen to another's pain and feel happy? *Yes, it is!* It is because I am not happy for that person's pain, I am not belittling it of ridiculing it in any way. , in fact I am holding a container for her to express it fully and it is not getting on me! I know myself to be an empath, someone who picks up the emotions of others and I have often had a hard time extracting myself from them. I am also a channel, and the openness of being a channel has, in the past, made it difficult for me to truly separate myself from the energy that I channel. This is a boundary issue, and I used to choose solitude in order to get back to feeling myself. So this was a new understanding, a realization that all of this work I have done to ascend my frequency, through excavating the Dark Seed, reprogramming my limiting beliefs, basking in the divine, and finally, integrating my twin flame, has truly paid off. I can now hold strong and be securely grounded in my column of light while hearing and allowing another person's pain. I am no longer a victim of my own leaky boundaries, of my desire to be and say and do the right thing. I just am who I am, and I am enough, and I don't need to heal anyone else or fix anything to be good enough. I just am.

And so are you. This is the reason I am sharing all of this information with you. I want to share my wholeness with you and I want to inspire you into realizing your wholeness. If you don't do the work or don't "get it," that's okay. If you do, well that makes my heart happy. Not because I need you to get it, but because I want to share this feeling of peace. I want the world to know the peace that passes understanding. Even as I am trying to write it in a way that can be understood, words will never do it justice, because it just *is*. This is where true, unconditional love begins. Realizing your wholeness is what will take you into ecstatic states of bliss, spiritual ecstasy, and divine rapture.

Integrating the Twin Flame

My twin flame integration experience was unplanned and unexpected. It was a very mystical experience for me, one that I didn't realize was possible until it happened.

I thought I was in Mount Shasta to co-facilitate a five-day retreat. I received a call on the morning that the presenter of the retreat was due to fly in. Due to some very strange and unexpected circumstances, he had to push the retreat back one week, which meant that I would no longer be able to facilitate because I was going to Hawaii. I had about a minute of, "Oh no, now what am I going to do with the next five days?" And about as abruptly as the thought came, it was replaced with "Oh *wow*, I have five *free days* in Mount Shasta!" So, I quickly packed up my belongings, traded my rental car in for a Jeep Grand Cherokee 4x4, and headed up the mountain to the highest area I was allowed to camp at. I set myself up to have a deeply spiritual meditation retreat on the mountain, and I had no idea that I would have the most profound spiritual experience of my life so far.

I spent several days hiking, communing with nature, meditating, and playing my medicine drum in the woods. I met some beautiful people. A friend came up the mountain to visit for a day, and we encountered a light ship, the first one she had seen, and it was undeniable, a blessing from our star family, which was also seen by two new friends with whom we were discussing our star origins as the brilliant light appeared to us from between the trees high above us.

My twin flame integration experience happened two days later. I was having an experience of spiritual rapture, inspired by a very deep meditation in which I was completely embodied by the Goddess Isis. Isis, through my body, sent out a call to all of her people, whom she addressed as Lemuria, that went something like this...

"I am Isis, hear my call! Lemuria -hear my call, this is *our world, our* 5D!

"Claim it!

"Claim it!

"Claim it!

"Claim it!"

As Isis was yelling out the call to her people, the call to claim back our world for the 5th dimension, I envisioned and sent the frequency of the earth as the 5D (and above) reality that it is meant to be, that it *was* and *will* be again, I envisioned the Ascension of frequency for *all* people of the earth and sent out my call with such intensity, such powerful feeling that there was absolutely nothing else that could possibly exist in this energy. I sent the call on the crystalline grid around the earth, and it carried the frequency of my plea, invoking the hearts of my people, the Lemurians, and I could see and feel them receiving the call and standing up in their courage and power to take action and reclaim this reality. I sent them the template to restore our grid, our frequency, our world, it was the most powerful call to action possible and I felt them receive it, more and more of them felt the call and responded, they stood up, opened their hearts and *claimed it* back, our beautiful Lemurian paradise, I saw it filling in the blueprint, the template was restored, great numbers of my people, they responded from around the earth and beyond, from all dimensions of time and space! The angels and archangels joined the call, we reached a tipping point of open hearts claiming our reality back as I yelled,

"Birth it!"

"Birth it!

"Birth it!

"Birth it!"

And *BOOM!*

The entire reality burst open... *we did it*! We restored the 5D template and birthed our world!

And I was reborn into *God*. And I was with God, and I was God. There was no more Isis or me, there was only God then, and it was me. Not me as my personality, but me as the totality of everything that ever has been, was or will be. All that is. I *am*.

There was a sound. It wasn't actually a sound though; it was a frequency that held it all together. There was no "it" so that isn't the right word, but all existed in frequency. It was white light that contained everything. There was no separation, only oneness. The feeling was beyond feeling. There is no human feeling that can describe it. I have heard people use the terms love, bliss, ecstasy, and rapture, however, even those words can't describe the feeling of unity with oneness because it was beyond any of those feeling states, and yet it contained every possible feeling or emotion. It was *presence*. Pure presence of totality. The ultimate wholeness.

From that beautiful wholeness emerged a new being. This luminescent being came to me adorned with shimmering golden robes and golden crown. She shown with a bright golden energy emanating from within her and projecting out around her. Her body was visible but not solid. She appeared to be beyond matter, yet composed of substance. She was more than a goddess or an angel. She was the essence of purity, completeness, and peace. Being in her presence was baptism into Divinity, just having her there was rapturous, and there was no time, she was the essence of presence, eternal now, there was no possibility of anything other than being present with her. In her majesty, I felt no fear, only bliss, and I surrendered to her completely. I released any questioning and all resistance. Those things were not necessary in the presence of Divinity. She spoke to me then.

"I am Christis. I am the Christed Isis. You birthed me when you became Isis and birthed the new world. Isis was also reborn and became one with Christ Consciousness, and now I am coming to you in gratitude for your service, and to share with you the true purpose of why you are here.

"I am not masculine or feminine, but rather a perfect union of integrated divine masculine and feminine energy. I speak in a feminine voice because it is nurturing and balancing to your soul. I am the essence of love and power. All within me is balanced."

She continued but not with words. Her communication became entirely telepathic through frequency and sound. I had on headphones playing beautiful music. Christis entered into the music and became pure frequency. I then experienced synesthesia, as the music transformed into substance, the substance of Christis. I could see the music as fractals, sacred geometry, as endlessly colorful, beyond any earthly color spectrum. I could feel the music as the notes rose and fell, and reverberated through my body, each sound carrying the substance of thought, emotion, color, and form. I felt the substance of Christ Consciousness, of Divinity itself, filling my body with light and energy as I saw the fabric of my form become crystallized. My crystalline blueprint turning on, my DNA being activated, the codes of creation being reignited and calibrated within my multidimensional human being-ness. I was in a state of total receiving and allowing. There was no resistance in me, as I silently expressed my delight and asked for more.

I was delivered into the essence of Divine Rapture. I was in my body but also everywhere, experiencing so much more than the third dimensional world. Two eyes emerged from the synesthetic fractal of colors. I recognized these crystal blue eyes set in a face with a beautiful smile and dark hair. I recognized him, it was my twin flame, the masculine counterpart to my feminine self. I had seen him many times before, and I was so delighted to see him now.

"Come to me!" I beckoned. Our eyes locked and the energy between us began to build and the pressure expanded us, similar to how it had felt when Isis birthed into God.

And then, with so much intensity and power, we merged into one being. We became a spiral, DNA, a helix of spinning energy that rose up to the stars, and then came down, piercing through the crown of my head and straight into my heart. My heart opened and

I saw the caduceus with the twin snakes, the kundalini rising to the top of the golden rod, and then my heart exploded and burst into wings, my heart had wings and could fly and I felt free!

Then I saw a dagger, it sliced my heart open even more, and in one massive burst of energy, I was reborn! My heart filled with the white light of the Divine, I was transformed, I was free, I took a massive deep inhale and it felt as if I had never breathed before that moment. All of the constriction of the past had been released, and I could breathe, and I was free! "This is what freedom actually feels like," I thought. "I have never known freedom before this moment!"

I had integrated my twin flame. The divine masculine and divine feminine of my being had united within me to make me whole again. I understood, that while I would still be a feminine expression of my *self* like Christis is a feminine expression of the Christ energy, I would no longer feel the yearning, the desire for someone outside of myself to complete me. I realized that I had been searching my whole life for this experience of completion, for this divine union that was within me the whole time. I realized that I had been looking for relationships with men to somehow complete me and fill a void that could only be completed by integrating my twin flame. Every relationship issue I had experienced made sense to me now because there was no way another person could fill a void that came from missing my own divine masculine. I also understood that this was all exactly as it was meant to be. I had chosen to experience incompleteness so that I could understand the wonderful feeling of wholeness, and so that I could understand other people's feeling of lack and yearning for completion, and help guide them to their own twin flame integration.

My relationships have changed since this experience. I am currently choosing to be single and continue to work with my inner essence and twin flame energy. I am upgrading, calibrating, and aligning to this higher truth. I understand that when the time is right, I will be "matched" with a partner who has my twin flame energy and with whom I can continue to grow and open into this work. Source has shown me that this will happen when the time is right. I don't need to go looking for it. If I want to date, I can, but I will know when I know, there will be no hesitation and the energy between us will be clear. In the meantime, I am happy. I have never felt so content and centered. I feel complete. I don't need to go looking for someone to fill a void within me because there is wholeness where the void used to be.

The twin flame integration is an embodiment of the *frequency* of your twin flame, your divine masculine or divine feminine counterpart. The process to integrate the twin flame is much the same as the embodiment of any characteristic, as you learned in the embodiment chapter.

Focus on your wholeness and the characteristics of your twin flame. Ask your higher self to attune you to the frequency of your twin. Practice integrating your twin flame frequencies in your daily meditations. It is much more likely that you will experience a gradual integration rather than the explosive sudden integration I had. There is no right or wrong way to experience the integration. You can use the Creation Codes of intention to go from intention to birthing your integration. If you are in a primary relationship, you can code your current relationship to be one of balanced masculine/ feminine energy. You have the tools to embody the frequency of your twin flame, integrating it to become a "match" to your divine masculine counterpart. When you do this, you will feel the wholeness within you. You will also have the frequency that will create magnetic attraction to your twin flame energy, so whether you choose to be alone or in a relationship, you will draw to you the people and characteristics that embody your twin flame energy.

CHAPTER 11:

———

Wholeness Makes You Irresistible

Anchoring Divinity: The Infinite Expansion into Christ through the Heart

Y ou are divinity expressed in a human form. You are not the human form. You *have* a body but you aren't the body. We identify so strongly with our bodies that we say things like, "When I die" instead of "When my body dies" or "The dog bit me" instead of "The dog bit my body or my hand" or "I'm fat" instead of "My body is fat."

The human form is an amazing tool, a Divine gift that we can cherish and optimize. It is a highly

———

advanced space suit that we use to navigate this world in. We get to experience amazing things in this life that wouldn't be possible to experience without a body. Isn't it worth it to optimize the human experience to the highest possibility, to feel and experience as much as we can with our bodies? In the grand scheme of things, we are only embodied in human form for a moment, so let's make the most of our human moment.

I have discussed ascending your frequency, through using the various techniques and also through storytelling. The story is an attunement embedded with Activation Codes. Scriptures are written as attunements, and sharing stories as a verbal tradition of handing down the history of lineage, as most cultures used to do before we began writing them down, is a way of passing down the lineage codes from generation to generation. I have always been a storyteller, and I have always felt the activation codes embedded in stories. You can see the faces of your listeners light up when listening to a good story. Our voices are encoded with frequency, and a storyteller's voice can completely change the receiving experience of the codes. Think of Morgan Freeman and James Earl Jones with their deep resonant bass voices that carry the frequency of sound right into the listener's cells. For this reason, it is important to be mindful of the stories we listen to. Stories hold the power to bring us up or take us down. The news is overflowing with negative storytelling. Those negative stories can enter your psyche and your body and create chaos.

I turned the news off 23 years ago and I haven't missed it. People tell me what I need to know, and the rest doesn't penetrate my life and bring my frequency down. That is one way that I buffer myself from absorbing the negativity of our society. When I watch "programming" on a screen, I choose informational or uplifting content. I do not watch horror and very rarely dark comedy. Because even if you enjoy the thrill of it, it is penetrating you on multiple levels and then you carry the frequency of fear. The frequency of fear becomes embodied through watching negative programs, through stressful work conditions, listening to certain types of music, through familial and societal storytelling, even though the food you consume and often you aren't aware of it. Then you wonder why you get sick, or why you have anxiety, or why you're short tempered. Thoughtforms are frequencies too, and being around people who think negatively will inevitably have an effect on you. The good news is that you can buffer yourself from all of this negativity, and you can choose not to participate in it. If you want your frequency to be higher, start eliminating the negative frequencies from your daily life.

If you want to upgrade your nervous system to be able to hold higher frequencies, you must eliminate negativity and fill yourself with positive. Choose positive people and groups to be with, instead of watching the news you can watch informative YouTube videos or positive shows, or better yet go to live theater or art museums. Practice a hobby you enjoy, exercise, or learn something new. Eat high vibe food. There are endless ways to enhance your daily life without indulging in negativity. Protect your frequency.

I have talked a lot about the experience of bliss, spiritual ecstasy, and rapture. These experiences are now a part of my daily meditation ritual. You only need to experience bliss or an ecstatic state one time to know the frequency of it. If you have ever had a climactic peak bliss experience then you have already had an attunement to a high-frequency experience and you can use that in your practice. If you haven't had a peak bliss experience yet, focus on a memory of a time when you felt your absolute most blissful. Whatever reminds you of the highest sensation of bliss or ecstasy that you can remember is what you need.

Remember the experience of your peak bliss moment. What did you feel in your body? Your mind was probably shut down. In very high-frequency experiences the mind shuts off and stops thinking. You are fully in the present state of now, and the experience is all there is. Recall in every possible detail the feeling you were experiencing. Recall the vibration of sound, light, color, emotion, physical touch, and any other detail from the experience you can fill in. Now make an energetic memory imprint of the frequency. The frequency holds all of the information of that divine moment in an energetic vibration that you can memorize and tune in to, like a radio frequency. Make a mental and physical imprint of the frequency and store it in your body and mind so that you can return to it often.

If you have had multiple experiences of ecstatic states, you can do this for each one, or put them together in one big frequency container, a radio station that plays all of your bliss moments, and you can tune in to it in your morning and evening bliss ritual. The next step is to begin your practice. You may want to create a bliss setting for your ritual. I practice mine for thirty minutes before I go to sleep at night when I am already lying in bed. I play either high-frequency music or listen to a spiritual book on Audible or YouTube. You may dim or turn off the lights, make sure you are comfortable, and tune in to your Bliss station. This is a time you are setting aside only to feel and bask in high-frequency feeling states. Make sure you set yourself up not to be distracted. Turn off your phone and computer, close the door or put up a "do not disturb" sign. Use this time to expand yourself.

Tune in to your beautiful diamond heart center and practice feeling. That is all you have to do. Just practice feeling good. It doesn't need to stay in your heart center, let your entire body receive the feeling experience. Ask the Ascension frequencies to work with you and help you feel more. If you notice yourself feeling afraid or shutting off to feeling more, practice surrender, and ask your body what it needs. Use the tools from the previous chapters to release your blocks. Do whatever you need to do to help your body feel bliss states. If a memory or an upsetting emotion comes up, great! Celebrate it; you just discovered a block. Whether it is a limiting belief, emotion, stored trauma, shadow program, or something else, work with it and go into contemplation, listen to it, ask it what it needs. Become the reporter and take a non-biased view and ask questions until you get to the core of it. Then release it. Feel it and release it. You have the tools to do this.

Here is the thing... the more you begin to feel, and the higher the bliss states you are able to experience, the more your old traumas and shadow programs will bubble up to the surface, because they can't stay buried in these high-frequency states. The higher you vibrate, the more they bubble to the surface as if you are boiling water and those old programs are bubbles- they must rise. And your job is to let them and release them. When you are in a high emotional state, it is much easier to forgive and release old patterns. Use this time to practice, and do not judge yourself if something dark shows up, accept it as part of the experience, celebrate it, and let it go, then go back to bliss. Practice this every day, and you will ascend your frequency very fast. Do the release work and you will be soaring through the cosmos of your expanded heart. You will upgrade your body and mind to receive and hold higher frequencies and higher consciousness. This work will lead to your spiritual gifts opening up, you will feel lighter, happier, more open and aware. This doesn't mean that you will never feel pain, regret, or negativity, but you will have the tools to recover much more quickly when those emotions come up. Whenever you get "pulled out" of your bliss state, tune back into your heart center and begin again.

You are anchoring Divinity within your body. Your body will upgrade; your mind will purify. You will release old ways of being and you will feel more alive, more yourself. You will begin to care less about what other people think and honor your own ideas more. Your creativity will skyrocket. Your relationships will improve, especially your relationship with yourself. And as you raise your vibration through these practices, you will inevitably become magnetically attractive to your energetic match. In love, in life, and throughout the Universe, all that is a match to your frequency will be irresistibly drawn to you. That's how it works. In anchoring divinity, you realize that you are divine.

Enjoy this expansion. Master your bliss. You are infinitely Divine!

CHAPTER 12:

Holding Space for Transformation

"The way we do anything is the way we do everything."
– Martha Beck

You have heard some of my wild and mystical stories, and you may think the reason I have been successful in my spiritual opening is that I am special or gifted, or some version of that story. You may be using that story to tell yourself that you aren't gifted in the same way so you won't get the same results... so why bother, right?

If you are telling yourself a story in order not to do the work, then I have a surprise for you: the only way you won't get results is if you don't do the work. It has nothing to do with being special or not or going to Mount Shasta or meditation retreats. I am not any more special than you are, but I am tenacious. I have been doing spiritual work for thirty years. Even though it seems like I "popped" in an instant, I had those experiences mostly because I learned to surrender, and when I learned to surrender, I kept surrendering. I will tell you that my results are 100 percent tied to my tenacity in doing the work consistently and surrendering more. That is what it takes, and I know that with consistency and surrender, you can too, and you don't need thirty years. I've seen people have incredible breakthroughs in a few weeks.

You have made it through this book, from mindset to wholeness, and hopefully everything in between. Now you have a choice to make. Will you do the work? Will you dig up the Dark Seed and transform it, planting a fresh, newly programmed reality for yourself? Will you practice the meditations that accompany the chapters? Will you integrate your twin flame and realize that what you have been looking for has always been with you? Or will you finish this book, put it on a shelf, and never think about it again?

Most people quit because they don't believe they can, and they don't want to experience failure. Maybe you've taken 100 self-help and energy work courses but you still have the same problems. Maybe you have a story or a program telling you none of this mystical mindset silliness works. Or maybe you have done some of the mindset work and the meditations, but you keep experiencing triggers and upsets in your life. This indicates that you haven't fully excavated the Dark Seed. You probably have some powerful programs guarding that shadow program and convincing you that this just isn't working. But it is working. Remember, courage leads to confidence, and the more courageous you are in confronting your triggers and shadow programs, the closer you get to finding the peace and love you so desire.

When you practice recoding, surrender, embodiment, holding the frequency of the twin flame. and traveling into the heart portal your life will transform... it must! It is a Universal Law, change your inner reality and your outer reality will change to reflect your new inner experience.

When you break through, this work will free you from worry, repetitive negative thoughts, and anxiety. You will experience a new level of energy and vitality, lightness, happiness, and openness to love. You will expand your love of self, self-confidence, self-care, and nurturing your heart. Finally, your twin flame will arrive, and you are so happy already that you maintain your inner peace with or without a relationship.

The way you do one thing is the way you do everything. Have you noticed that? It takes commitment and tenacity to make real change, and you can do it if you choose to. You have everything you need at this moment to change your life for the better, to ascend your life, to realize your dreams. There is a lot of mystical content in this writing, but there are also a lot of action steps that must be physically done in order to recreate your reality. Will you do the work this time?

This is where your mind will try to stop you with thoughts like, "I'm too busy, I have to do (__fill in the blank__) first," " I'm too (old, young, right-brained, dyslexic, lazy, unhealthy, ADD, etcetera) to complete this depth of self-awareness, I want someone else to do it for me." The truth is none of that is true. Do you want to change your life or not? That is the only question that matters. If you do, you can. You have the tools to begin right now, maybe you already have and you are already seeing results. I believe in you. I know you can do it. You can do it yourself; you can do it with a partner or a friend, you can do it with a circle or meditation group. But you have to do the actual work yourself.

If you really want to do it, and you feel you need support, you can do it with me. I have a program that can help you get through the process with the support of myself and a group of people who also want support.

The statistics say that eighty percent of people who read this book will never do the work. That leaves twenty percent of people who will. Most people don't reach their goals because of mental roadblocks, the same blocks that keep you from completing anything you've started in the past will come up again and try to stop you. The blocks that sabotage your goals and your dreams, that argue that there isn't enough time or money, or that you aren't a good meditator will try to stop you.

Many people will quit. If you listen to your shadow programming, you will quit. But what if you don't stop this time? What if this time you keep going? Even when your shadow programs come up, what if you take a courageous stand and work with them, listen to them, excavate them, and reprogram them once and for all? What if you aren't the person who gets stopped anymore? I stand for you to be that person. I am right here, in the pages of this book, holding space for you to be the person who confronts your self-sabotaging limitations and transforms your life.

Will you continue to constantly look outside of yourself, feeling victimized or "at effect" of your life, experiencing loneliness and yearning? Will you let addictions and addictive behavior make choices for you as you are ineffectively trying to fill that internal void?

I've been there, I've done that, I've felt that pain, and it's torture! It's self-torture, and it is a really sad place to be. The idea of you staying in that state, of anyone staying there and missing out on the outra- geously delicious experience of this life in this body makes me sad. But you are only torturing yourself because you don't realize that there is so much beauty waiting for you on the other side of that void. Now you know better, and when you know better, you do better, and you can begin to fill that void right here, right now by committing to yourself and choosing a higher path for yourself. This is your life. You only get to live this life now, so why not make the most of it and go for it? You can go all the way and experience the embodiment of bliss, right here, in this body, beginning right now. When you feel that, the all-encompassing expansion into oneness, there will be no more self-sabotage. You will know the truth of who you are, you will feel and express your divine truth, and you will expand your connection to the Divine, to other people, to all of creation. You will ascend.

CHAPTER 13:

Knowing Love

The *ASCENDING SPIRIT* does not get bound
by anything
"When you are loved, you can do anything in creation. When you are loved, there's no need at all to
understand what's happening, because everything
happens within you."
– Paulo Coelho

It is a vulnerable thing to be loved and to let the one you love see the truth of who you are. To let someone hold your heart in theirs, to allow them to know you deeply, to see into your life, your heart, your innermost world. Allowing yourself to be loved is to open up the hidden world where you question your worth. It is opening the box where your deep truth lives, that place where you are raw and real, and to let it be seen and known for all that it is, even when you fear being judged. We as romantics crave that type of love. The unconditional kind that doesn't judge, that loves us despite our quirks and flaws. We seek it, we yearn for it, we aspire to be worthy of it. If only we could find it. Does love like that even exist, or is it just the subject of princesses and fairy tales that we desperately want to believe in?

It does exist, I assure you! It is woven into the fabric of our world, in every great story, play, and poem, in the waves of the ocean and the rays of the sun, in the rainforest and in waterfalls. Love is the very energy and frequency that holds the matrix of our reality together, and we feel the truth of it in the depth of our hearts. When we surrender to this knowing, we open not only to love but to *being* loved.

Thank you for taking this inner journey with me. I acknowledge you, I appreciate all of your efforts, I celebrate your expansion, and I recognize your divinity! This work is a journey of self-discovery and unfolding that I hope becomes a lifeline and a guidebook, a recipe to ascend your experience of living this life in the body you are in. What I want for you more than anything is for you to know that you are not alone. You are deeply loved, you are whole, complete, powerful, and Divine!

When you practice these concepts, do the meditations, witness and work through your triggers, expand into the heart, and keep surrendering to the embodiment of your upgrades, you will realize that the power to create worlds is within you. It always has been. You have everything you need. You don't need another training, another teacher. All you need is to open your mind and your heart and know that your divinity is within. When you open the sacred portal of your heart and you allow yourself to travel within, collecting your soul codes, expanding in your ability to embody and hold higher frequency states, you will feel a new freedom, a new gorgeous connection to what you always have been, to your own oneness with Divinity! Your heart holds the creation codes for you to transform your life.

Work with your triggers, release the bondage of your mental prisons, all of the limiting thought-forms that you have been absorbing since birth can be cleared. When you courageously work to excavate, acknowledge, clear, and reprogram your Dark Seed, you will know yourself in a new, expanded way. The small and invisible part of you will fall away. You will no longer feel the need to protect yourself from the judgment of the world because you will know that the judgment you were feeling was only a part of yourself that you hadn't yet healed.

When you surrender your deepest darkest fears and you allow your spirit to guide you, you stop resisting, stop fighting for your own limitations and surrender to your inner power, you expand more. As you keep surrendering, you keep expanding. You will see a thread of humor in the way you bought into the falseness of your own lack of mentality. You will realize that death is an illusion, the soul is immortal because it is the very consciousness that exists in everything that is. You will begin to truly know yourself as unlimited. What will you inspire your reality with, what will you manifest, create, and eliminate from your current experience? You get to choose.

You will have the courage and the openness to connect with others, to share the essence of your heart and the radiance of your being with the world. When you integrate the twin flame within you, you will feel a wholeness that you could only imagine before. Your heart will truly be free, you will no longer relate to others from need, every relationship will be one of joyful exploration and heart connection. You will be able to breathe in a new way as if it is for the first time, and your breath will not be constricted. It will be full and complete and charged with the frequency of the divine, filling you with more light and love as each breath is your intimate connection to your Divine truth of being.

As you bring the essence of your new expanded fullness into your body more and more, you will feel more than you have ever felt before. There will be new energy, more colors, details, and a new crispness to life. The melancholy dullness of the world before will seem like a dream that you have woken up from. You will be effervescent, bubbling with life, and ready to share it with the world.

This is your awakening. No matter how many times you have awoken already, know that there is more. There is always more. There is infinitely more. Be tenacious in your exploration of expansion and your deepening into your divine truth. You have the entire multiverse working on your behalf to assist you in your ascension.

You don't need to find another class or teacher to do everything I have shared in this book. That doesn't mean that you have to do it alone or that you can't have the support of friends and community. If you have a friend or partner to practice with, that's even better. You can do your work simultaneously and share your successes and failures (with are only learning experiences) as you expand.

Sometimes, it really helps to have a guide on your journey. You may get stuck on a trigger, you may not always have the drive from within to keep doing the work. I get that, it happens to me too.

If you want support and assistance in your process, I am here for you. I am your ally and I can assist you when you get stuck or need a coach to help you through a block. You can apply to join my Ascension Training program, which will take you through the steps in this book with my assistance, guidance, and support along the way. I dive deeply into each of the steps in Ascension Training, unpacking them even more along with weekly activations and meditations that will guide you to the places that are often difficult to navigate on your own.

Community is essential. To know that others are also on this journey of expansion with you is heart-warming and uplifting. Having others to share the journey with is something that many of us as spiritual seekers have been missing, which is why I encourage you to join my Facebook group "Ascension Training with Waxéla Sananda." If you desire to dive into this work in person with me, I offer workshops and retreats for the embodiment and expansion of all that I have shared in this writing. You can practice deepening your connection to the divine with me guiding you, along with like-minded community, and you are sure to create lifelong friends and reconnect with members your soul group at these life-changing embodiment retreats.

Visit my website to learn about upcoming trainings and events.

Acknowledgements

I have been intending to write a book for many years, but to finally sit down and have the focus to complete it was daunting for me. I'm a great starter of projects, finishing is often my challenge. I had to choose the life of a hermit in the months that I was writing, and I am grateful to my friends and family for supporting me through the process, and for being there when I emerged from my cocoon.

I am so grateful for my parents, who accepted my unconventional, rebellious, creative mind from the beginning. I know I provided many challenging moments, I still do, but your unconditional love has provided a safe foundation for me to explore my multidimensional mind.

I feel truly blessed by my fourth-grade teacher, Ruth Ann VanDonslear. You are one of the treasured, special teachers that cared so much. Your kindness taught me more than anything I've learned in books.

I acknowledge the unique and unforgettable team of Divine Mothers who were there in my early twenties, supporting my greater awakening in Kauai,

Hawaii and beyond. Ileah VanHubbard, Dawna Su Maria, and Peggy Watson. Thank you also goes to Michael for holding the Divine Masculine center in that sacred time and place.

Thank you to Blake, you opened my heart and placed a love there that I will never forget. You are missed.

Thank you to Jerushua, for pulling me out of Dallas and escorting me the way through the portal, where the multidimensional truth of my being was waiting to show me who I really was.

I have so much gratitude to Joren Kinnetz for guiding me through multiple QHHT sessions that helped me unlock the hidden contents of my mystical experiences, my multidimensional and past lives and level up my awakening so that I could share more clearly, confidently, and openly with others.

My gratitude goes to Janine Gustafson and Yoga Okoboji for bringing me in toward the beginning of my "coming out" publicly with my intuitive work and spiritual teaching. You create such a beautiful, welcoming space for the expansion of mind, body, and spirit in a place where it can be risky to stand for such things. You were a pioneer in the Iowa Great Lakes and I will always appreciate your faith in me.

Thank you, Ayn, for always being a true friend no matter how much time passes in between connecting. I love that we can always pick up where we left off.

Brett, thank you for supporting me for the last 14 years of this journey. You have always held space for my spiritual expansion. You are an amazing father to Gabriel and I am grateful for our ongoing friendship.

I would not be the person I am today without my amazing children, Josiah and Gabriel. Josiah, you are changing the world with your devotion to cleaning up the environment. But your greatest gift is your huge heart. Your presence lights up every room and you are destined for great things. It is so exciting to be your mom and watch you grow.

Gabriel, you bring smiles to everyone who meets you. You are a joy, remember to lead with your heart and the world will be at your fingertips.

I am eternally grateful to my Ascension Training clients, for giving me your trust and faith and for letting me see the impact of my work on other people's lives. It is my greatest joy and accomplishment to see the work touch, enhance, and expand others.

To my Dr. Joe Dispenza community... the work and expansion we have experienced together have changed my life in so many ways. I am grateful for those who have become dear friends and for every single person who I have sat with and shared a conversation with at the retreats.

To my online communities on Facebook and Instagram, your support and feedback warms my heart and brings me so much joy.

And finally, to my brother Alex, who I know is watching from the great beyond. His love and bear hugs continue to guide me on.

About the Author

Waxéla (wa-shay-la) Sananda is an activator of Spiritual Gifts, Ascension Trainer, an embodiment of the Divine Light Codes, a clairvoyant psychic empath and an avid explorer of spirituality and consciousness.

She is a channel of light frequencies that activate the latent spiritual gifts and soul codes within her soul family.

Waxéla works with her clients in multiple dimensions, creating and holding space for each one to receive exactly what is needed to move into a higher state of awareness, and to clear old blocks and patterns, transforming stagnant energy into dynamic, creative possibility.

Using consciousness technologies, such as the Lucia Light and Quantum Sound Therapy, Waxéla combines her celestial abilities and shamanic training to design quantum consciousness shifting experiences.

"My mission is to assist people in achieving a greater level of consciousness, upliftment, and inner peace in accordance with their highest good." ~Waxéla

Find the meditations that accompany this book at: https://waxelasananda.com/TLYC

Website: https://waxelasananda.com/

Thank you

Thank you for reading *The Love You Crave: A Course in Ascension, Alchemy, and Connection to the Divine*. It is my greatest joy to share my heart and my spiritual work with you. If you use any of the tools, techniques, strategies or stories in this book to improve your life then I have succeeded in my purpose for sharing this work with you.

I have recorded some free supporting meditations that you can access at https://waxelas-ananda.com/TLYC

I am sending you so much love and I am holding space for your Ascension journey.

Namaste,

Waxéla Sananda